"The authors are true pioneers in fostering creative processes for visioning. This practical guide provides leaders at all levels with tools and perspectives that can help a team, a department or an entire organization to shape tomorrow, together. It enables innovative forms of dialogue and sets the stage for the collaborative design of preferred futures. *Creating Futures That Matter Today* fills an important need in leadership literature that emphasizes the importance of visioning but often provides few practical roadmaps. This book helps to fill that gap."

Juanita Brown Ph.D., Co-Founder, The World Café

"By following the unique methodology in *Creating Futures that Matter Today*, I was able to facilitate a powerful visioning experience that helped senior leaders in our company explore and align around a new future state. During the visioning, differences in perspective were treated with curiosity and hierarchy fell away as everyone connected around how much they care about our company's future. With the shared vision as a backdrop, follow-on conversations and business planning processes were more passionate, focused and aligned both on the business needs and the culture required to reach that vision."

Lori Costew, HR Lead, Ford Smart Mobility

"This book is an essential guide for any senior leader or consultant who needs to help an organization get out from under the day-to-day of short-term priorities and instead, design and implement meaningful, powerful and effective organizational futures. It shows us a path through some of those seemingly impossible business moments when it's either change or become obsolete. This book is a must for all leaders who want their organizations to remain relevant in the future."

Barbara Spencer Singer, CEO of Executive Core

"As someone who has followed the authors' work for many years, I am extremely impressed with the clarity and usefulness of this book! The impact on people in so many different organizations has been immense – not just in financial and growth terms – but also in catalyzing creative human talent to discover and design more innovative and meaningful organizational futures. Their work has made a real difference, and now, by reading this book, it is your turn!"

Dr. Scott G. Isaksen, Professor, Norwegian Business School (BI)

"For the past 20 years, the authors' shared visioning methodology has been a key differentiator in our award-winning cross-disciplinary Agroecology M.Sc. program. By teaching our students this approach, they are able to facilitate shared visions across multiple stakeholder groups and can intervene at a systems level without becoming bogged down in details. Using the tools described in this book, they acquire the practical know-how and courage to facilitate important changes through shared vision. Most definitely a book for educators, as well as leaders and consultants!"

Geir Lieblein, Professor, Department of Plant Sciences, Norwegian University of Life Sciences

Creating Futures
that Matter Today

Facilitating Change Through Shared Vision

Anna Pool & Marjorie Parker

futures
that matter

Executive Savvy, Inc.

Creating Futures that Matter Today: Facilitating Change Through Shared Vision © 2017

ISBN 978-0-692936-84-9

Cover design and illustrations by Andrew Kim

Typesetting by Book Polishers

Edited by Zoë Harris and Kate Coe

Published by Executive Savvy

34 Lewis Mountain Lane, Durango, CO 81381

www.futuresthatmatter.com

Printed in the United States of America

First Edition, September 2017

We dedicate this book to all our clients, past and present. Your willingness to try something entirely new to bring about positive and meaningful organizational futures continues to be incredibly inspiring and gives us hope for the future.

Contents

Introduction

You may think of envisioning the future as some lofty, idealistic process that doesn't really have much practical application. But, what if visionary thinking could be a key differentiator for you as a business leader, consultant, coach or educator?

Whatever kind of change facilitator you are, be it business or NGO leader, internal or external organizational development consultant, leadership coach, trainer or educator, you already know the importance of inspiring change around critical organizational challenges. But you may be tired of investing energy, time and money into change initiatives that are difficult, if not impossible, to implement due to a lack of organizational focus and alignment.

There are many books that explain the "whys and how" of creating and formulating a vision statement for your organization. Likewise, there are a number of books advising how to create a vision for yourself. What's missing, however, is a deeper understanding of the real possibilities and impacts of visionary thinking as an approach to proactively addressing change. This book will fundamentally reframe the possibilities for how visionary thinking and the creation of shared visions can positively impact an organizations' ability to facilitate change. This book is about accessing the collective intelligence of a team to identify challenges and discover new opportunities critical to the future of your organization. It will show you how to access both your team's and your own innate creative capacity to envision relevant, achievable solutions to these challenges – solutions clear and motivating enough to provide a framework for making decisions today.

We believe there are three core needs that are driving and will continue to drive an increasing interest in facilitating change through creating shared vision. These are the need for leaders and their teams to experience a greater sense of meaning and connection in the workplace; the need for stronger alignment and focus around a desired future state; and the need for leaders to shape a work environment that supports creativity and innovation. In our experience, visionary thinking and creating shared visions around challenges that matter has powerful and positive impact on these three needs.

By helping teams lean further into their intuitive, creative and imaginative capacities, more powerful futures can be designed. Accessing the full capacities of the brain provides a remarkably practical approach to strengthening a team's response to the many leadership and organizational challenges driven by today's volatile world.

Our intention is to arm you with tools and strategies for facilitating change through engaging your teams and stakeholders in creating, communicating and implementing shared vision, whether the changes are large, medium or small. For example, how can you engage your team's capacity for visionary thinking in the re-design of a production facility? Or how to refocus your organization on its customers in a meaningful way that really does positively impact their day-to-day experience? Or, how can shared vision be an effective approach when responding to an imminent crisis, one that threatens to shut down a key piece of your business?

While elaborate strategic planning processes may give a sense of control over the future, they often do little to actually build alignment and commitment to it. They frequently fall short of being inspiring or meaningful. Shaping a compelling future happens best through full engagement with the desired future, supported by genuine inquiry and powerful conversations that authentically awaken people's desire to commit. We have observed that most people really do want to commit. The desire to step up, engage more fully and take more responsibility is often just waiting to surface. Respecting talent by engaging them in a visioning process sends a powerful message that we all have the power within us to discover solutions to our most pressing challenges and to take steps to turn our visions into today's reality.

We start this practical step-by-step guide with an overview of some key terms, like vision, shared vision, visionary thinking and the difference between goal setting and creating shared vision. In Chapter Two we focus on helping you identify opportunities to use visionary thinking in your organization and we share actual examples that illustrate the many kinds of challenges that have been well served by this approach. Chapter Three identifies the steps needed to lay the groundwork for the shared visioning process, and in Chapter Four, we guide you through the all-important process of writing a script for fast-forwarding your team into a desired future state. We suggest types of questions which can free teams' imagination and stimulate relevant images of new possibilities.

From there, in Chapter Five, we explore how to facilitate the team from their individual visions into one shared vision. And finally, we focus on making the vision real: how to use creative thinking to ensure that the vision is successfully adopted and implemented. Our final chapter discusses the longer-term impact of facilitating change through shared vision.

This guide and the tools in each chapter will help you to engage your team more fully, solve some of the challenges that keep you or your clients up at night, and develop a true spirit of innovation in the organization.

Let this book stretch your thinking about what is possible – for your teams, your organization and for yourself as a leader, consultant, coach or educator interested in generating and implementing creative and powerful designs for organizational futures that matter today. We hope you enjoy the journey!

Chapter One

Introducing Vision

Understanding Vision

If you ask a group of fifty leaders, "How many of you consider yourselves visionary thinkers?" how many hands would go up? In our experience, not that many. Most leaders don't consider visionary thinking part of their skill set. While many leaders recognize the need for it, most lack an understanding of what that entails. This has resulted in a focus on formulating vision statements, rather than experiencing visioning. Leaders and change agents need to better understand the nature of vision and what enhances and sustains it. They need to access their own and their team's capacity to envision relevant solutions to the critical challenges facing their organization today.

People experience vision differently. Most experience vision as mental images; some experience vision audibly, hearing it as words; still others experience vision intuitively as feelings. Some people experience vision in all these ways. We have observed that, most often, in an organizational context, visions are experienced and talked about as mental images. Visions are powerful mental images of what we want to create in the future. They are a product of our imagination, our insight, and our values. They reflect our sense of purpose.

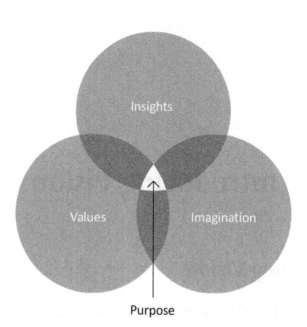

Figure 1: Where our visions come from

However, a vision is not somewhere out in the ether. While a vision directs us toward the future, it exists only in the present – in our minds, right now. The tension we feel when comparing a mental image of a desired future with today's reality fuels the vision. Without an ongoing awareness of today's reality, visions become powerless. The visioning process creates a magnetic field with the pull being away from today and toward the future. The magnetism of a vision is generated from the integration of an individual's and an organization's sense of purpose, values, uniqueness and interaction with the physical, social, business and political environments.

Visions are the deepest expressions of what we want to create. They are compelling and they provide an overarching framework that guides us in making choices – choices that will transform our visions into new realities.[1]

---

1   Parker, Marjorie. Creating Shared Vision – The Story of a Pioneering Approach to Organizational Revitalization. Clarendon Hills, Ill: Dialog International Ltd, 1990.

Shared Vision

Creating and aligning a team around a future that matters is one of the most persistent challenges leaders face. Typically, change efforts require a high level of engagement from an organization's people. Diverse groups of stakeholders must come together and agree on what the future should look like. Change expert John Kotter uses the term 'change vision' to describe a picture of the desired future, once the change has taken place. In his words, "Every successful large-scale change that I have seen has, as a part of it, a change vision. And what that means is a picture of after we have made the changes on whatever dimensions, this is what we're going to look like."[2]

A shared vision does exactly this – it provides alignment around a picture of what the desired future will look like. It unites and provides the link between diverse people, interests and activities. Shared visions are expressions of what people have in common; of what they, as a whole, are committed to. People with shared vision are more likely to take responsibility; they are more likely to challenge the bounds of convention.

Any group of people can create a shared vision; any challenge can be the focus of shared vision. When a shared vision has been authentically created, refined and communicated, the normal barriers and roadblocks to implementation fall away. People are excited about the future and are supported by the courage and connection to the larger group. Silos and 'us vs. them' mentalities lessen, replaced by commitment, communication and action.

---

2 Kotter, John P. "How to create a powerful vision for change". Forbes, June 7th 2011. Accessed June 2017.
http://www.forbes.com/sites/johnkotter/2011/06/07/how-to-create-a-powerfulvision-for-change/#4cfc40fd2a3c

Visionary Thinking

In business or strategic planning processes, we tend to pay attention to information attributed to what is typically ascribed to our left-brain functions, such as analytical thinking, reasoning, logic and language. When planning for an unknown, uncertain and complex future, this is often not sufficient. We need to reach further into our intuitive, creative and imaginative capacities. Visions are about imagining and bringing into being new possibilities. In order to create genuine, lofty, challenging shared visions around specific challenges and opportunities, we need to increase our capacity for visionary thinking.

We describe *visionary thinking* as the process whereby we activate our insight and imagination, connect with our values and sense of purpose, and create mental images of a desired future state relevant to the challenge that is in focus. With a leap of our imagination, we mentally 'fast forward' into the future and allow ourselves to see what is going on around us, sense what is happening, how we are feeling and what is different and unique in this new individually desired reality.

Pehrson and Mehrtens, in their book *Intuitive Imagery*, describe what we call visionary thinking as a whole-brain approach. "It [the whole-brain approach] works by bypassing the dominant left brain and its rationality to allow the more intuitive right brain to 'speak' through images and feelings. Because these images come from deeper levels of awareness, they can transcend emotional attachments, fears, anxieties and habits of perception that limit what we see and know. Once the right brain has been allowed to speak through images and feelings, the left brain is re-engaged to interpret, validate and apply the information received."[3]

The literature is full of anecdotal evidence citing the power of the whole brain. For example, one of the most popular TED Talks, *My Stroke of*

---

3   Pehrson, John B. and Mehrtens, Susan E. Intuitive Imagery – a Resource at Work.Newton, MA: Butterworth-Heinemann, 1997

Insight by brain researcher Jill Bolte Taylor[4], speaks of her personal experience of accessing the other functions of her brain during her experience of a stroke that shut down her rational left brain. Her reports of her ability to access increased intuition, empathy, creativity and insight are compelling. And more neuroscience research comes out daily, citing the powers of integrated brain functioning.

Visionary thinking enables communication between the conscious and unconscious levels of the mind. It provides simultaneous access to both levels. This encourages the subconscious to find possibilities that may be below conscious awareness. Whether or not we envision a future that is relevant, meaningful, inspiring and makes sense in a business context is dependent upon the questions we are asked to respond to.

> **Visionary thinking enables communication between the conscious and unconscious levels of the mind. It provides simultaneous access to both levels. This encourages the subconscious to find possibilities that may be below conscious awareness.**

Can we harness the power of visionary thinking to design organizational futures that matter today? Our fifty years of combined experience tells us unequivocally, "Yes!" Companies like McKinsey and Google are investing heavily in mindfulness training to ease stress, augment focus and build empathy in their key leaders. It's no surprise, then, that visionary thinking now can take its rightful place among the many processes and tools employed in the design of futures that matter today. Visionary thinking can be used whenever there is a need for change. Without it, new ways of thinking or acting are inhibited by the pull of the status quo. As leaders and their teams sit together to create shared visions, very specific and practical images of that future guide the way forward.

---

4   Bolte Taylor, Jill. "My Stroke of Insight". TED Talk, TED 2008. Accessed June 2017.
    https://www.ted.com/talks/jill_bolte_taylor_s_powerful_stroke_of_insight

What Are the Differences Between Goal Setting and Visionary Thinking?

People often ask us, *what is the difference between goal setting and visionary thinking?* From our point of view there are some fundamental differences between goals and visions that affect how we think and feel, as well as the actual impacts of each approach and the underlying assumptions that guide them. These differences have significant implications on many levels.

How We Think

Thinking in a goal-oriented manner stimulates analytical and logical brain functions. Goal setting leans into a more convergent thinking style at the expense of divergent thinking, thus limiting the exploration of options and creativity. Convergent thinking is most useful in a problem-solving or planning process when creative options have already been fully explored and it's time to narrow the solutions to a few of the best.

Thinking in a vision-oriented manner supports a divergent approach to thinking and allows the group to fully explore and discover more possible futures. Visionary thinking stimulates the full functioning of the brain, allowing access to mental images and intuitive knowing. The group can more easily grasp the whole picture and how all the pieces are interconnected. Using divergent and convergent thinking in the right ways, and at the right points in the process, stimulates creativity and allows for the possibility of breakthrough solutions.

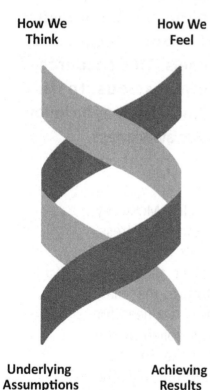

How We Think

How We Feel

Underlying Assumptions

Achieving Results

Figure 2: Differences between goal setting and visionary thinking

How We Feel

When we work in a goal-oriented frame-work, we tend to ask questions like: *What do we have to do in the next two years?* Or, *What do we have get better at?* Then, we often come into contact with our own sense of insufficiency or lack of resources. We ruminate on the feeling: *Now, if we are any good, we have to achieve [xyz] . . .* For example, think about a time when you set a personal goal for yourself, maybe to ex-ercise more or lose weight. Were you excited and inspired, or dutiful and determined? For many people, personal goal-setting is not very enjoyable and can even be intimidating or stress-provoking. Follow-through and success rates are typically quite low.

> **When we work in a vision-oriented framework, the visions are immediately inspiring because they are a result of responding to the question, *What do we want to create?***

How we feel when setting organizational goals is not much different. Often, the goals have little personal relevance. Achieving them may or may not be motivating. We may feel a sense of duty to achieve results, but find it's hard to feel any real excitement, passion or internal commit-ment to make them happen.

When we work in a vision-oriented framework, the visions are immedi-ately inspiring because they are a result of responding to the question, *What do we want to create?* They come from an internal drive, which springs from the recognition that more is possible. When we are invited to envision what we want to create, we are aware of that which we care most about. We express meaningful values that are intrinsically inspiring at an emotional level. Our imagination is automatically stimulated and we come into contact with our own and our group's creativity and sense of purpose. The experience is refreshing, rejuvenating and often exciting.

Underlying Assumptions

Assumptions are the beliefs that influence our emotional reactions, our choices and our behaviors. They are the hidden software that drives our experience of life. Often, they are unexamined and unknown to us. One of the key assumptions that seems to drive the goal-setting process is that if a leader gives a team a goal, or if a team identifies a goal, it will happen. For example, if an organization's sales and operational leaders meet together and set a goal of achieving a certain amount of revenue through a new cross-selling initiative, the assumption is that it will be achieved.

Experience shows this is not so. Setting goals may be adequate in the context of a team that is facing an unchanging future, if this even is possible anymore. But, when groups need to work, for example, in a cross-boundary manner, such as sales and operations, setting goals is rarely sufficient. In order to activate the new ways of thinking and behaving that will be necessary to activate cross-selling, more is needed.

When working in visioning mode, the assumption is that together the group needs to seek new possibilities with intention and purpose. They need to explore, learn, listen and create a shared vision that provides direction. As Moss Kanter[5] says, the group needs to take a leap of imagination and faith together. The change vision must be illuminated and owned by all.

Achieving Results

As the starting point for goal setting is an analysis of today's situation and our reaction to it, goal setting could be described as a reactive way to relate to the future. Goals are made from what we know and what we feel is possible today. As such, they limit new thinking and constrain possibilities. This approach works well for situations that don't require a new way of thinking about or relating to a challenge. But, most disruptive change requires that the team undergoes a transformation in its own mindset

5 Moss Kanter, Rosabeth. *Change Masters.* New York: Free Press, 1985

and discovers something that is completely new. Goal setting cannot provide this.

After a goal is formulated, the attention goes immediately to dividing it up and making action steps. It's easy to shift the focus from the substance of the goal to focusing on how to reach it. Teams are often overwhelmed by all the isolated action steps and lose sight of what the goal actually was. This process of dividing the goal up into steps further isolates and polarizes team members. Each one has his or her piece of the goal to implement. Without a shared vision for the change, new siloes are created or existing siloes are reinforced. The 'us vs. them' mentality continues and the new goal will not provide much help in addressing the problem.

A visioning approach is not constrained by the present or by current reality, but instead seeks to proactively seek out what is possible. Visionary thinking stimulates the subconscious to look for possibilities that may lie below conscious awareness. It works beyond the rational, the linear and the logical, and offers a bigger opportunity for the team to ideate around. In this way, visionary thinking opens the possibility for results that are far beyond what a standard goal-setting process can provide.

Goal Setting	Creating Shared Vision
How we think	
Stimulates analytical and logical brain functions	Stimulates mental images and intuitive brain functions
How we feel	
Dutiful	Inspired
Determined	Energized
Disengaged	Passionate

Underlying Assumptions	
Less focus on exploring and sharing underlying assumptions	Must actively explore and share underlying assumptions about the challenge
Achieving results	
Goal is typically a re-hash of past solutions	Heightened possibility for break-through futures
Low levels of alignment and commitment to implementation	High alignment and commitment to implementation

Figure 3: Summary of differences between goal setting and visionary thinking

Conclusion

In this first chapter, we have provided an overview to help you understand the most important concepts that are fundamental to creating futures that matter today.

In Chapter Two, we get very practical and share numerous examples of how creating shared vision has worked in discovering more ideal solutions to critical challenges confronting organizations of all sizes and also offer some reflections on what made the process work. Our intention with this next chapter is to inspire you to begin to identify opportunities for using visionary thinking within your own organization.

Chapter Two

Addressing Organizational Challenges Through Shared Vision

When an organization faces the need for change, whether it is a hospital's need to rethink how it manages patient intake or a multi-national corporation that needs to revitalize and reinvigorate its core values, the question, "How do we accomplish this?" naturally emerges. Typically, a few people are called together and a brainstorming or planning process is used to come up with some alternatives. Or, one person is tasked with creating a proposal that usually includes identifying the tradeoffs in various options for moving forward. Often, however, the stress and pressure of the day-to-day lead a single leader to make somewhat arbitrary decisions based on constraints like time and cost.

There are many hidden and not-so-hidden costs to this approach. The failure of the change effort to provide the solutions that were needed can quickly become obvious. For example, the new patient-intake system may have solved a few of the most glaring problems, but it soon becomes apparent that many of the same problems, such as unacceptably long waiting times and the lack of a quiet place for administering paperwork, are still unsolved. And, despite an internal marketing campaign full of value-oriented bling, office contests and recognition programs, the multi-national's core values are not assimilated or aligned around the change in the manner that is imperative for business success.

Clearly, finding and using methodologies that both leverage the full possibilities for a group's creative thinking, and unite and align stakeholders around how to move forward are critically important. Whether large or small, public or private, organizations can't afford to continue to fall short in their ability to fully envision the possibilities for an important change.

Our purpose in this chapter is to demonstrate, through sharing several examples of change initiatives, the varied organizational and leadership challenges and opportunities that this approach can effectively support. Taking the time to engage a group in a manner that allows it to bring the full potential of the whole brain to the table brings powerful insight and unleashes opportunities that were simply not accessible through traditional planning processes.

> **Taking the time to engage a group in a manner that allows it to bring the full potential of the whole brain to the table brings powerful insight and unleashes opportunities that were simply not accessible through traditional planning processes.**

We begin by sharing a case study describing the use of visionary thinking in an organizational crisis – one where a production unit of a major Norwegian industrial firm was threatened by headquarters with an unexpected and immediate shut down. We're starting with this case to quickly reshape any beliefs you may hold around the efficacy of creating shared visions. It's not just a fun teambuilding exercise for use on a sunny day when things are already going well. Quite to the contrary; the process can be especially relevant in a crisis, where a shared vision must be quickly identified and acted on. Following the story, we will analyze the learning points.

As background, we should mention that Marjorie has lived and worked in Norway for many years and the mini-cases we present here are based on her experience with Norwegian corporations, health care institutions and government agencies. Her methodology for leading groups in facilitating change through dialogue and visionary thinking was developed in the early 1980s, and was inspired by her American colleague, Juanita

Brown, participation in the International Women's Dialogue group, the work of Peter Senge and MIT's Organizational Learning Center, and the International Center for Studies in Creativity in Buffalo, NY. Although the examples are from Norway, the organizational contexts and processes described are equally applicable to other countries and cultures.

The Story of a Leadership Team Facing Crisis

This is an actual scenario which Marjorie shares here, but organizational details have been changed to protect confidentiality.

It was an icy cold Thursday morning in January. I had taken an early morning flight from Oslo to Trondheim, Norway. I had just gotten off the elevator on the fourth floor of the executive office building of one of my clients, a major Norwegian industrial plant. Typically, upon my arrival at this plant, I would be met by the welcoming smile of one of the directors, offered a cup of coffee and a pastry, then led to a meeting room.

This day was different. I walked into the reception area of the executive offices and noticed that the doors to the offices were closed. I sat down and waited. Suddenly, the plant's managing director appeared, looked at me with a somewhat strained expression.

"Be with you in a minute, Marjorie, we've got a little crisis here," he said, then disappeared into another office. After a few minutes, the vice president of operations swished past me, a nervous smile on his face.

"We will be meeting in my office, Marjorie, but I have to send off a couple of emails first. I also have to have a word with our finance director," he said.

I sat there, beginning to feel the tension in the air.

"What's going on?" I asked myself.

Before I had time to begin guessing, the senior vice president of manufacturing emerged, looking extremely agitated. Talking through an open door into another office, I overhead phrases such as "We just cannot afford a strike," "Headquarters doesn't understand our situation," and "To close down that part of the plant now would be disastrous!"

I could feel indignation rising within me. I knew these leaders – I cared about them. Could it be true that corporate headquarters was ordering them to close one of their business units? I was aware that part of the plant had been facing some financial challenges. I'd heard rumors that there might be some operational problems. Some felt that the competency of the management team in that unit could be better. All this was true, but still, why now? The company was in the middle of a large-scale revitalization effort. Management and union leaders were well on their way to finding solutions to these challenges.

All three of the directors with whom I was to meet were clearly preoccupied, frustrated and angry. I thought to myself, "Marjorie, face it, it's not realistic to expect that these men will be able to focus on the agenda we planned for today. Get up, go quietly out the way you came in and take a taxi back to the airport."

While preparing myself to suggest this to them, they suddenly appeared together, all three huddled together, outside the door to one of the offices. From where I was standing, it sounded like they were all talking at the same time and blaming themselves as well as bombarding each other with ideas about what should be done. I overheard statements like, "We have got to do this!" "No, we have to be careful about – !" "If only we had done this two months ago!" "Why was I so stupid that I didn't –" "This couldn't have happened at a worse time!" "You should call –" "No, bad idea. They don't know what they're doing," "If only you had –" and on, and on.

I interpreted the occasional forced smiles that were cast in my direction as a signal that, yes, Marjorie, they know you're there. They're feeling a bit guilty about keeping you waiting, but they're facing a major crisis that's much more important than anything else right now. Watching them at a distance, I recognized how much compassion I felt for them. I stood up and went to them.

"You all are obviously upset and I wish I could help. Let's forget the agenda we had agreed upon for today's meeting. If you are willing, why don't we sit down in one of your offices?

Maybe together we come up with some strategies for dealing with the situation," I said.

These three directors knew and trusted me. Still, from the astonished look on their faces, I was sure they were thinking: "Marjorie, our dear consultant, *you have no idea what we are dealing with!* We don't have time to sit around and hope for some intuitive revelation! We must act, *now!* We're worried about a couple of hundred people that might be out of a job very soon." Although a bit unnerved, I heard myself reiterating that I thought it might be worth a try. They looked at each other, sighed, and said, "Well, okay, we can take a half hour."

We all went into an office with four comfortable chairs. I borrowed a laptop and told the executive assistant that I might be emailing her a document every now and then, and could she please print it out and return it to us immediately. We quickly agreed to what we hoped would be the desired outcome of the meeting: to come up with a realistic alternative future for the business unit – an alternative that could convince corporate headquarters to reconsider its decision to shut it down.

Relaxation

My first challenge was to get the three directors into a relaxed state of mind. Because the situation they were dealing with was both complex and emotionally charged, I knew from experience that starting off with a relaxation and brain-quieting exercise would be far more effective than leaping into a discussion or brainstorming. Being in a quiet state makes it easier to harness the power of the imagination. It allows for easier access to intuitive insights. As they were all feeling considerable stress, I guided them through a body-centered exercise that helped them slow down their minds, focus on their breathing and come more fully into the present.

Envisioning Outcomes

I wanted to avoid the natural tendency in this kind of situation to quickly generate and toss ideas around and then make hasty judgments for dealing with the ultimatum from corporate headquarters. To help them access their values and knowledge, and stimulate their imagination, I sensed that envisioning the business unit one year ahead in time – a unit better, more efficient, more productive than today – could be a start. I trusted that guided imagery would be the best approach given the situation. Once they were in a relaxed state, I asked them to continue to keep their eyes closed and imagine that it was January, one year ahead, and the unit was a prime example of a well-functioning, efficient, productive and positive workplace.

To stimulate images of this optimal future business unit, I described first one scene or situation and then another. I asked them to imagine themselves being present in these situations and then posed questions to stimulate their insights and imagination.

As I made up these scenes, I kept my eyes closed. The following is the gist of what I said:

"Keeping in mind that it is January, one year from now, imagine yourself standing in front of the entrance to this unit. Imagine yourself walking into the reception area. Look around. What do you see? What do you hear? Share aloud with me the images that appear in your mind."

I asked them to imagine standing on the roof of this extraordinarily effective and well-functioning business unit. I asked them to look down through a hole in the roof and examine the entire layout of the whole unit. What do they see? Where are the various facilities placed in relation to each other? How are the production lines organized?

I led them on a walk through the building and asked them to take photos of places that showed new technological breakthroughs. The three directors, still with their eyes closed, responded by describing the production flow and logistics. They spent time exploring how relocating key pieces of machinery and equipment could enhance the overall production efficiency, from materials origination to final product creation. They explored the improvements that had enhanced employee safety and the overall working environment. Together, they shared images of how employees were interacting and how key values such as trust, openness and quality were manifesting in interactions between employees.

An image in one leader's mind would trigger an image in the minds of the others. Each one's images seemed to build on the others and the picture of the unit became increasingly detailed, yet also holistic. The three leaders had long since ceased to be agitated. No time was spent blaming anyone for the crisis or finding scapegoats. They were focused, relaxed and concentrated, and they seemed excited about sharing their images as they emerged. They did not censor one another's images, but took an appreciative approach to each person's ideas.

I invited them to imagine being a senior leader in a multinational company in the UK – a company that bought products from this very successful Norwegian company. I asked them to imagine preparing an editorial for the in-company newsletter at the UK company that explained why they had just signed a long-term contract with the Norwegian manufacturer. Why are they so pleased about this contract? How is this Norwegian unit providing them with added value? They described what the Norwegian business unit was offering, from the perspective of the UK customer company, which better helped them serve their own customers.

Gradually, after about one and a half hours, we all agreed that what they had envisioned was sufficient. The images of the three had coalesced into a working draft of a comprehensive shared vision of the business unit. It embraced innovative new elements that ensured their unit would be fully capable of functioning efficiently as well as providing a positive working environment for its employees. I had kept extensive notes about the images that had emerged, and when the executive assistant handed back the printout from my notes, we had in our hands a four-page detailed description of the business unit as they wanted and felt it could be in one year's time.

Imagining Stakeholder Responses

Although the three executives felt very excited about their visions of the business unit it was important to develop it further. I queried them who their main stakeholders were and then asked them to mentally move in to the role of these stakeholders and look at the possible consequences seen from different perspectives. So, again in a relaxed state, and with eyes closed, I asked them to imagine being the CEO at their corporate headquarters. What was it about this future business unit the CEO would find appealing? What would he find to be of benefit for the whole corporation?

I invited them to take on the role as mayor of the local community, then as director of another business unit in the same plant, and then as spokes-man for an environmental organization. In these roles, they first imagined the positive consequences for themselves and those they represented, and then their concerns. Although this was a rather primitive mini-conse-quence analysis, it provided information that helped them make improve-ments and modifications to their initial vision.

Generating Evaluation Criteria

The next step was generating possible criteria that could be used to eval-uate and prioritize the various aspects of their vision. Although they were convinced at a gut level that their vision of the unit, one year on, would gain support, I felt it important to test it against criteria. For example, would the new business unit require investments that would negatively impact other agreed-upon priorities? Was there time enough to train or develop key personnel? Did the unit, as envisioned, contribute to overall business goals? Was it compatible with the values espoused by corpo-rate and plant management? Using these kinds of criteria, they carefully evaluated their vision to ensure that it was strong, clear and relevant. Going through this process led to some adjustments in their vision and strengthened their commitment to it.

Imaging a Communication Strategy

Knowing how quickly visions and new ideas can be judged and knocked down by those who have not been a part of creating them, I asked them to imagine who all the people and groups were that would likely support and could assist in making this vision a reality. Then, what people or groups might resist? A discussion followed of the best process for gaining interest and acceptance for the vision as well as how to constructively deal with possible resistance.

I asked them to once again imagine being the CEO. What kinds of questions might the CEO ask when he first explores the vision? What would his concerns be? What about the union leader? The directors imagined themselves meeting with various people and listening to their potential reactions, both positive and negative. Again, after a review of the printout from the executive assistant, additional modifications were made.

In the final part of the meeting, I asked them to mentally move into the future once again (one year ahead in time) with their eyes closed. The new business unit was a reality. They were asked to look back from that future time and imagine: What were the first steps they took to gain acceptance for their vision of a different and better business unit? How did they, as a management team, go about communicating the vision? How did they go about communicating the benefits of the changes that needed to take place? How did they respond to the fears of certain individuals and groups?

Analysis

After almost four hours, we concluded the meeting. There was full consensus among the three leaders, who were excited and committed to taking immediate action. They felt calm and confident that they could convince corporate headquarters to change their decision to close the business unit. I was pleased, too. From time to time during those four hours, I felt I was fumbling – unsure of which questions were most pertinent. Now and then I said to them that I needed a couple minutes time-out. Then, I would close my eyes and imagine how best to proceed.

I left for Oslo on an early afternoon plane, leaving the managing director at his desk, editing the notes from the meeting to send to headquarters. I was exhausted and my neck hurt from bending over the computer. On the plane back, I kept asking myself, what else should I have thought of? What other questions should I have posed?

At eight o'clock the next morning, I got a phone call from the managing director. He seemed truly elated. He told me he had been informed by headquarters that he had the go-ahead to take steps toward making their vision a reality. The business unit would not be closed. One and a half years after this meeting, I read in the company newsletter that this business unit was the most profitable of all the corporation's Norwegian and European production facilities.

I remember very clearly all three directors saying to me as I left that afternoon:

"This is a whole new way of working! Why haven't we done this before? We don't have to use visionary thinking just to create a lofty vision of our whole company. We could use it to address any number of our current challenges!"

Reflections

It's clear to us that several elements positively influenced the success of the outcome in this specific case study. We have reflected on these below in two categories we believe are the most important for success: the mindset of the leaders and the mindset and skill of the facilitator.

The Mindset of the Leaders

The mindset of leaders plays a crucial role in a successful visioning process. But what exactly is mindset? Defined as "the established set of attitudes held by someone," a leader's mindset can either play a powerful role in enabling the effective use of visionary thinking or it can completely derail the entire process. Carol Dweek, the author of *Mindset: The New Psychology of Success,* distinguishes two types of mindset: the fixed mindset and the growth mindset[6]. People can display either at different times, depending on the setting and the issue.

A fixed mindset is one where the leader believes that he or she is already an expert, knows what needs to happen next, and doesn't need the input or involvement of others to be successful. Often, it is a comfort zone that one simply prefers not to stretch outside of. In situations where collaboration or new learning isn't needed, it isn't much of a problem. But because so much of today's business requires collaboration and learning, it is quickly rising to the surface as a barrier in change initiatives.

A growth mindset is characterized by the desire to use every opportunity to learn, not just technically but also about oneself, gaining insight into how one impacts others, why he or she reacts in certain ways, and how they can accelerate their growth and learning. Those with a growth mindset tend to collaborate more easily and comfortably, seeing value in what others can offer.

To stay in a growth mindset required for facilitating change through shared vision, there are a number of things a leader must do.

---

6 Dweek, Carol: *Mindset: The New Psychology of Success.* New York: Ballentine Books, 2006

A Leader Must Show a Willingness to:

· Find an alternative solution

When leaders feel an emotional connection to the need for a solution, it often motivates and inspires others to share in that commitment. If a challenge doesn't inspire some level of passion and emotion in the organization's leaders and teams, it may not be an appropriate focus for creating shared vision.

· Maintain an experimental attitude

Because it is truly impossible to predict outcomes prior to engaging in the visioning process, it's important to have an open mind, allowing one to think, "Well, we don't know for sure what, if anything, will come out of this, but it's worth a try."

· Move into a relaxed state of mind

Being in a relaxed state of mind improves one's ability to image. Nothing productive can emerge when our minds are racing with our concerns and to-do lists. Leaders and teams must be willing to engage in one or other form for relaxation before envisioning a desired future state.

· Be open to whatever images emerge without judging or negating them

We are taught from an early age to judge and rank much of the world around us, as well as our internal world of images, thoughts and feelings. The ability to suspend that tendency, even briefly, in the visioning process allows us to tap deeply into our inner world of imagination, intuition, values and feelings. Harvesting these provides rich fodder for designing the future.

- Suspend the tendency to get practical right away

Being willing to enter the world of possibility is essential. This allows space for something entirely new to be imagined and explored.

- Listen deeply to, and build on, other people's ideas

An open-minded and inclusive mindset inspires out-of-the-box thinking, enabling new ideas to be explored and developed.

- Think creatively about implementation

The need for creative thinking does not end with sharing images of a desired future state. Criteria and plans for testing it, exploring consequences and gaining support for it and communicating it to key stakeholders are critical to its success.

By imagining a desired future state from various perspectives, and from different stakeholders' perspectives, more and more information becomes available, which helps develop and refine the vision. The failure of change initiatives often stems from the lack of clarity and specificity about what the desired future state or outcome should, or could, look like. Engaging leaders in designing the future state from various perspectives ensures a level of detail that makes both communication and execution of the vision much more viable.

To Be Most Effective, the Facilitator Should:

- Create a safe atmosphere

Create an atmosphere where participants feel safe enough to close their eyes and become open to visualizing and sharing their images.

- Work from the assumption that the leaders themselves have the knowledge they need to create a meaningful and compelling vision

In other words, a facilitator doesn't need to be an expert on the organization or its industry, but should understand the basic principles of the challenge the visionary thinking is focused on to be able to formulate relevant questions that elicit a wide range of images. Visions allow us to see more of the whole, both from a detail point of view and from the perspective of how all the parts fit together.

- Have a basic knowledge of factors that enhance visionary thinking and creating shared vision in a group

In most situations, a crisis is not looming and there is time to prepare the appropriate future scene and questions for the visualization. It's also important to know how to help the team identify important criteria, think creatively about possible sources of acceptance and resistance, and think about alternative action steps – all of which help to improve an initial vision and strengthen commitment to it. The purpose of this book is to prepare you to lead exercises like this.

- Be willing to take a risk and not know what the outcome will be

There's always the risk that when you move into the unknown, the team might not find their desired future state. In our experience, that has happened extremely rarely, but the facilitator must be willing to risk it.

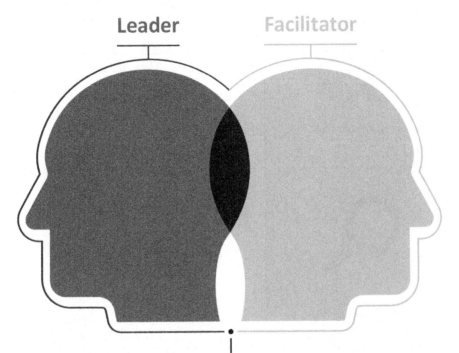

Leader   Facilitator

A leader must be willing to..

Find an alternative solution

Maintain an experimental attitude

Move into a relaxed state of mind

Be open to whatever images emerge without judging or negating them

Suspend the tendency to get practical right away

Listen deeply to, and build on, other people's ideas

Think creatively about implementation

A facilitator must be able to..

Create a safe atmosphere

Work from the assumption that the leaders themselves have the knowledge they need to create a meaningful and compelling vision

Have a basic knowledge of factors that enhance visionary thinking and creating shared vision in a group

Be willing to take a risk and not know what the outcome will be

Figure 4: Mindsets for creating shared vision

Re-thinking a physical space

Reinvigorating core values

Clarifying core purpose

Bringing a critical concept
or idea to life

Defining the ambiguous
opportunity

Identifying a new role

Engaging cross-functional
collaboration

Building customer focus

Figure 5: What Can Be the Focus of a Vision?

Examples of Opportunities for Envisioning Change

As the sidebar opposite shows, there are myriad opportunities and challenges that lend themselves to creating shared visions.

Envisioning the outcome of a project, a new function, a system, a course or a training program are also among the many situations that can be the focus of a shared vision.

In the next section, we have compiled a list of past projects that have been well served by a visioning approach. However, it is by no means exhaustive. We invite you to add to the list as you become proficient in leading shared visioning efforts.

Re-thinking a Physical Space

An out-patient clinic was faced with several challenges: unacceptably long wait times, an unattractive and noisy environment that created stress for patients and staff, and an unwelcoming entrance and waiting room that had an industrial and unfriendly feel to it. Overall, the effect on patients and their families was out of sync with the clinic's stated values. The leaders assembled a team of diverse stakeholders including intake staff, patients and key leaders. Together they envisioned their ideal waiting room and intake flow. They shared their images of the desired future state of their waiting room two years ahead in time. They saw a different and more effective layout, an aesthetically more pleasing interior, and a more welcoming and effective reception area. They shared and illustrated their future waiting room and made step-by-step plans to make it a reality.

Reflections

The use of, design or form of any physical space or geographic area can be the focus of a change vision, whether it is a reception area, cafeteria, factory floor, laboratory, a coastline, an entire building or location. By envisioning a desired future physical state, it's possible to capture the whole design simultaneously. You can invite a group to see themselves walking through a physical or geographic area, traveling over it in a balloon, sitting somewhere in it, or maybe observing the inside from a hole in the roof.

It is possible to envision all the details: a more effective layout, the colors, the interactions between people or the ways that a landscape appears when it is being well protected. This leads to very specific and deliberate design decisions around which there is broad agreement and excitement for implementation.

Reinvigorating Core Values

As part of a leadership development program, the top management of a large international corporation felt that the company should be more 'responsive'. They chose "being responsive" as one of their core values. They were led through a process where they:

- Reflected over and had a dialogue around what they consider is the essence of the word 'responsive'.

- Drew a mind-map of all the situations in which they and the company needed to be responsive.

- Identified whom they needed to be responsive towards.

- Discussed what they felt their competitors were especially responsive to that allowed them to be more effective and productive.

They then envisioned what 'responsiveness', manifesting two years in the future, would look like. They responded to questions such as:

- What are we doing differently today because this value is now an integral part of how we interact with each other?

- How are our customers noticing that this value is now core to how we behave as an organization?

They shared their images of what they saw happening and how they were being responsive in the contexts that were important to them. With these images as background, they visualized the steps each would take to make their departments' responsiveness a reality.

Reflections

Often, the leaders of an organization select a few values, and then roll them out to the company in the form of an email, wall posters or other swag. Involving employees and other key stakeholders in envisioning values manifesting in the future is a much more powerful alternative. We suggest that you begin with a dialogue session to create a deeper understanding of what is really meant by these values. We explain more about the use of dialogue in Chapter Three. Clarifications and alignment generated at this point set the subsequent visioning process up for success.

 ## Clarifying Core Purpose

The management team of a Health and Social Services Department was looking to clarify their core purpose. They held a dialogue in which they addressed the questions: "Why are we really here?" and "How do we want to make the world a better place to live in?" They decided that "to help people master their lives" was a deeper purpose that each of the separate functions could identify with.

The 240 employees in the organization were invited to envision how they would like this core purpose to manifest in the future. They chose a five-year perspective. After identifying the major user groups and clients they served, they imagined being a client in each of the different user groups, and envisioned how, in five years' time, each of these were better able to "master their lives." Then they shared their images with each other about what this core purpose could mean from their clients' points of view.

Afterwards, they again moved five years into the future and envisioned the capabilities and competencies of the organization – specifically, what was it about their services that enabled the clients in each user group to better master their lives? They envisioned what they were offering and how they were doing it. This process revealed areas of strength and challenges from the organizational capability point of view. The visions gave direction and focus for their strategic planning activities.

Reflections

Visionary thinking can be very effective in looking at how we want our core purpose to manifest in the future. Implications and impacts that might not be realized in a typical planning session are identified, understood and built into success criteria. In this example, the focus area, the organization's core purpose, was so mission-critical, the decision was made to include 240 employees in the actual visioning experience. This quickly built a critical mass of engagement and influence and helped ensure implementation and appropriate cultural shifts.

 ## Bringing a Critical Concept or Idea to Life

Construction projects initiated by a federal public roads administration are huge, long-term, complex and involve persons from a wide variety of departments and professions, such as project managers, civil and environmental engineers, national and local government leaders, and construction companies and workers. In southern Norway, the management of a regional authority felt it important for all its employees to have a holistic perspective on the construction projects. There was, however, no shared understanding of what this would mean in practice.

A group of key stakeholders assembled and were invited to envision themselves three years ahead in time. They were asked to share their images of how managers and project groups were interacting with each other and with users when all were working and collaborating from a holistic perspective. This was then followed by a discussion of what it was in their current situation that undermined and supported their ability and willingness to embrace this holistic perspective. Action plans were made to address these.

Reflections

This situation was complicated by the need to engage people around a totally new idea – to deeply understand and enact the concept of a holistic perspective. Clearly, a brainstorming process would not yield the insight, clarity and motivation that the visioning process did. Situations where a group needs to learn together, to create shared meaning around an opportunity or challenge, are ideally suited to the visioning approach. And, as we have discussed, so too are situations that require identifying a desired future state with input from diverse key stakeholders.

 ## Identifying New and Ambiguous Opportunities

The leaders and researchers from a department in a national transportation authority had the task of identifying research and development projects that would allow them to more effectively leverage technology and minimize the environmental impact of their transportation initiatives. When faced with an upcoming deadline for presenting proposals for new research programs for the next planning period, they identified a common organizational challenge: how could they perceive all the possibilities while also narrowing options down to a proposal that was both effective and attractive to the government funders?

The head of the department invited leaders and employees to an off-site workshop. They were invited to envision various parts of the country ten years in the future. They imagined travelling through various landscapes, villages and towns at different times of the year, and envisioned future solutions that spurred new ideas as to where further research in technology and environmental impact were needed. They then looked at these future solutions and analyzed which cross-functional competencies they, as a group, would need to develop these solutions. This was followed by defining the research and development projects for the next five-year planning period that would strengthen these competencies.

A major hospital was in the process of creating a new position for nurses. The position was to be called a 'nurse advocate'. One of the new functions connected to this position was serving as a patient-care coordinator, described as being the 'driving force' in complex patient situations to make sure that all providers were fully informed and would cooperate on behalf of the patient. The leadership team needed to create a new role description and training program for candidates to the new position. The concept behind the role was also new, and so the candidates themselves needed to get a shared understanding of what being a 'driving force' could entail.

They held a two-day seminar to envision what was happening, for the nurses, staff and patients, when the clinical nursing specialists were serving as a driving force in complex patient situations. Together, they developed a clear view of how this looked in practice. Their shared visions helped clarify which competencies were needed to fulfill this function and, in turn, influence the content of the training program.

Reflections

When a leadership team is faced with a strategic but undefined opportunity, whether it be the opportunity to imagine future research and cross-functional training needs, or the need to define and identify training content for a new role, visionary thinking can play a key part. The human brain has a startling capacity for understanding and engaging in the desired future state, when given the support and guidance to do so. In both cases, the teams could better understand and align around the future opportunities as well as analyze them to identify the competencies that would be needed for success.

 ## Engaging Cross-Functional Collaboration

The county authorities from eight different regions near Oslo met to explore ways to advance cooperation in the areas of infrastructure, education, environment, and hospital administration. They used visionary thinking in connection with each of these areas and imagined the nature of collaboration five years into the future.

Reflections

The need for collaboration across roles, governments, borders and ideologies has never been stronger. Visionary thinking lends itself to fostering connections, building relationships, and ultimately, helping to develop a desired shared outcome, regardless of backgrounds, professions, orientations or points of view. Simply sitting together and engaging in an authentic exploration of the desired future state begins to break down silos and barriers and offers new and motivating solutions to opportunities and problems. By putting themselves in the roles of other stakeholders such as customers, end-users, or other groups, people are more able to see others' perspectives, which leads to increased understanding and respect.

 ## Building Customer Focus

Three colleges (nursing, technical and office administration) in a large Norwegian county wanted to explore how they, with the help of one another's competencies and resources, could effectively integrate environmental studies into all three of their institutions. They first envisioned the capabilities and attitudes possessed by students from each of the three schools upon starting their first job after graduation. These shared visions gave direction and perspective as to what needed to be integrated in the curricula of the three institutions. The college representatives then decided how each school could contribute to the other two.

An institute at the Norwegian University of Life Sciences was concerned about the challenges arising due to the distance between food producers and customers. Researchers from the institute, farmers producing organic foods, representatives from the local communities and companies in the county envisioned what the situation could look like in the future when the problems of distance were reduced and cooperation between the stakeholders was vastly improved. Positive impacts at local and national levels were outlined and intended.

Reflections

The issue of how to better organize around customers' interests and needs is a common theme for leaders and organizational consultants. It's often not an easy initiative to be successful in.

Creating a cultural shift is one of the hidden potentials of visionary thinking. Whether the shift is on a small scale, as in the first example, or a larger one, as in the second, the principles of inclusion, alignment and creativity remain consistent.

Summary

As you can see through these examples, the use of visionary thinking has many applications. Whether you are trying to envision the design of a new space, create a new role that has never existed before, or are in a crisis that threatens to shut down your company, the approach provides many avenues for exploring the future. Leaders need to be alert to these kinds of opportunities and seek out situations that lend themselves to creating shared visions. Before you finish this chapter, we encourage you to jot down a few ideas that may have come to you as potential areas where you could facilitate change through creating shared visions.

Once you have identified a challenge or opportunity, there is some work to do to lay the groundwork for the visioning session. Creating the right environment, familiarizing participants with the process, and practicing skills like dialogue and guided imagery are all key to ensuring a successful experience. We will explore these in Chapter Three.

Laying the Groundwork

In this chapter, we explore how to lay a foundation for the shared visioning process. First, we focus on identifying opportunities for facilitating change through shared vision in your organization. Next, we talk briefly about dialogue – a form of conversation that enables people to look beneath the surface to discover the core assumptions underlining their thinking about a challenge or opportunity. We discuss the importance of creating the right level of urgency and building a coalition to drive and support the change. Assisting others to understand the benefits of shared visioning is key to this, so we've provided a simple exercise to help you see how to do this. Guiding your team to become more comfortable with relaxation and mental imagery is also important. We have included some example exercises to illustrate this.

What Can Be the Focus of a Vision?

As we demonstrated in the previous chapter, there is an endless number of challenges or opportunities that can be the focus of a shared vision. One way to identify an opportunity is simply to glance through this list:

- Re-thinking a physical space

- Reinvigorating core values

- Clarifying core purpose

- Bringing a critical concept or idea to life

- Identifying new and ambiguous opportunities

- Identifying a new role

- Engaging cross-functional collaboration

- Building customer focus

As we explained in Chapter Two, these are real life examples where facilitating change through shared vision has been the focus. Reflecting on the list may trigger ideas for opportunities that would benefit from visionary thinking in your organization. For example, you could ask yourself:

- Could we benefit from envisioning an ideal layout for the new physical facility we are thinking about building? What about its production flow or other aspects?

- We all agree that in our hospital our core value is 'the needs of the patient come first'. But might it be time now to review what exactly those needs are and envision new and meaningful ways of how we could meet them?

- We keep talking about the concept of transparency, but we don't walk the walk. Is this a concept we could bring to life by having a shared vision of what's going on when transparency characterizes our interactions with stakeholders?

- Where, within or outside our organization, is there a serious need for improved cross-functional collaboration?

Dialogue Around the Questions We Have Not Yet Asked

A second approach to identifying a challenge or opportunity is to invite your team to consider, "What are the questions we have not been asking ourselves – that have perhaps not been on the table for years?" The value of being genuinely curious and posing questions that move us away from what is already known to something we haven't yet discovered isn't always clear. It's often a big stretch to move from the first paradigm to the second. And yet, being willing to make that transition makes it easier to identify a meaningful focus for a visioning process.

There are many examples of the kinds of questions that can work as powerful stimulants to help organizations acknowledge areas where they need to change. Focusing on the biggest dilemmas facing the organization, or exploring the organization's key differentiators as compared to competitors, can be powerful. What product, service or process could benefit from some radically new thinking? What does your organization stand for? What do you, as a group, believe is your deeper sense of purpose?

Let's pause here and take note of the fact that there is some common context to questions like these. They are all questions that need to be reflected upon and explored fully. Why?

- No one person has the single right answer.

- The answers to these questions depend on inquiry, and on maintaining an attitude of curiosity.

- Many perspectives are needed to create coherent answers.

- The likelihood of experiencing breakthrough thinking is greater when members can articulate the core assumptions underlying their thinking.

- It's likely that everyone will learn something new, or see factors they already knew of from a new perspective, at some point in the conversation.

We have found that introducing some guidelines for dialogue, and giving a team the opportunity to practice them as they work towards identifying a possible focus for a shared vision, can benefit the process. Dialogue increases our capacity to listen for understanding. When participating in a dialogue, team members search for the strengths and value in others' points of view, appreciate how others' thinking can improve on their own and dare to pose questions that they don't have answers to.

Our experience is that once a team gives it a few tries and reflects on what went well, or what could be done better next time, team members discover how incredibly effective dialogue can be. Dialogue is useful for a team or group when:

- it's important to explore a question for which there is no obvious answer;

- when a problem keeps reoccurring despite previous attempts at resolution;

- when there is a need to change their way of thinking about an issue;

- when a group needs to have a deeper, shared understanding of an issue, a concept, an ambiguous opportunity, a value, a declaration or an initiative.

The guidelines for engaging in dialogue appear deceptively simple. Their practice is difficult, but powerful. Invite your team to look through the list of guidelines for dialogue and reflect on which ones might be the most challenging for them to follow. Then, following the first meeting, help them become aware of how they could practice it.

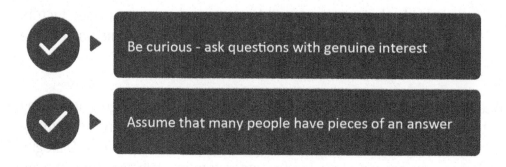

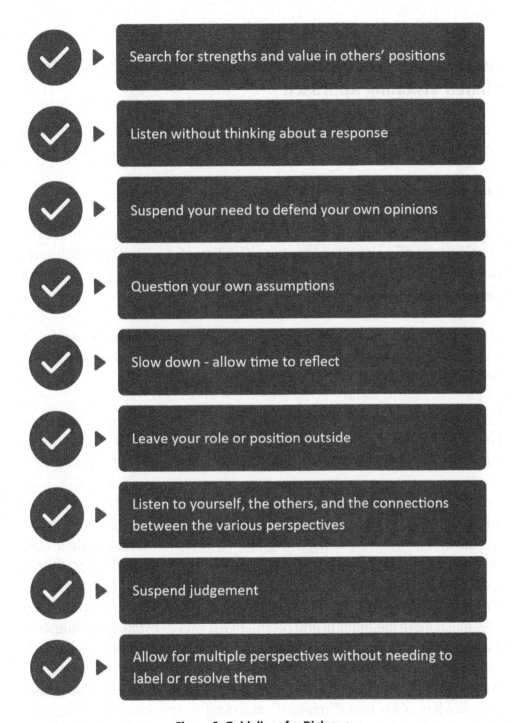

Figure 6: Guidelines for Dialogue

Using Dialogue to Identify and Clarify an Opportunity for a Shared Visioning Approach

Consider the following real-life situations where we have used dialogue to lay the groundwork.

Dialogue Leading to Envisioning Core Purpose

We were invited by one government authority to help them facilitate the development of a shared vision. In our first meeting with the director, we posed the question: "Could you tell us what you feel is your organization's deeper sense of purpose?"

The first response was, "Oh, that's written in our official charter when we were established twenty-five years ago. I'll check. I think it's in a file on the bookshelf over here."

He found it, looked at it carefully, and said, "Hmm . . . I can't recall if we have ever talked about this during my time here. I don't think the formulation here is what you are referring to when you ask about core purpose."

During a meeting with the other members of the leadership team, they all agreed that this was a question that they, as a group, had never really sat down and discussed. They also agreed that rediscovering their core purpose would be a better first step than focusing on creating an overall vision for the organization. The leaders were introduced to some guidelines for dialogue and, over a period of several months, they experienced how much more meaningful and productive it was to explore this question using dialogue rather than the form typical of Monday morning meetings.

They gradually aligned around a core purpose that both employees and stakeholders alike found relevant, meaningful and inspiring. Following this process, they then involved regional managers and their teams in envisioning their core purpose, manifesting five years into the future, in new and innovative ways.

Dialogue Leading to Envisioning Key Values

Management teams frequently participate in an offsite gathering to discuss the values they feel should characterize their organization. Our experience is that when groups of managers and employees engage in serious dialogue and explore what they feel is the deeper meaning of that value, in the context of their interactions within the organization and with their interactions with stakeholders, the value becomes much more than a nice word on a poster.

Afterwards, if the group envisions how they would like to see that value manifesting in the future, a fuller and more authentic adoption of the new value becomes easier. As the value itself comes alive through people's conversations and behaviors, posters aren't needed as reminders. In other words, engaging first in a dialogue to look beneath the surface and inquire, "What do we really mean when we say that *value x* is important?" is a critical first step. The next is envisioning it manifesting at some date.

Dialogue Leading to Envisioning a New Initiative

Leaders and politicians often come with announcements like, "It's time we become more flexible!" or "We have to be more customer-focused!", "We must become more change oriented!" or "More innovative!" These declarations may well resonate with those who hear them. They may be aligned with their values so that they think, "Yes, indeed, we should be that!" The problem, however, is that there is no shared understanding of what these words mean. What happens is that there is some general agreement about how important it is that they become more this or that, then a work team is established and action plans created. After a while, however, no one notices any changes and people become disillusioned. And when nothing changes, employees lose their trust in the leadership or whoever came up with the pronouncement in the first place.

It's much more effective to develop a shared understanding of these well-intentioned words first through dialogue and then work together to envision how they might manifest in the future. This greatly increases the possibility of the desired state becoming a reality. Our images of the future exist in the present, in our minds. When they are so real that they engage our emotions and our intellect, steps will be taken to make them happen.

> *"Using dialogue to access our collective intelligence around questions that impact our organizations is one of the greatest investments that leaders can make."*
>
> **Juanita Brown, author of The World Cafe**

Creating the Right Level of Urgency

Creating a high level of urgency is considered one of the basic tenets of solid change management. Often called a 'burning platform', it speaks to the importance of addressing the "why" in any upcoming change initiative. While we wholeheartedly agree that speaking to the urgency of the change is important, there are some other factors than come into play with this. The first is that of change fatigue. Most companies have been through years of multiple, significant changes, often at the structural, process, leadership, product or other levels. Typically, these changes have occurred back-to-back or on top of one another. Usually, they are driven from the top, with little or no input from the broader employee base. If leaders do get around to explaining why the changes are being made, the answer is usually something to do with increasing revenues or cutting costs.

Think about the impact of continual change from the viewpoint of the average employee. Change often causes work that was once simple to accomplish to become more difficult and take longer. It may require people to learn new behaviors, technology or skills. People and teams may lose connections with each other, which slows down efficiency and effectiveness.

Relationships that once energized and inspired people are lost, leading to lower engagement and absenteeism. Typically, old siloes get reinforced or new ones form. In the end, slower speeds and lower quality of work end up impacting the customer or product and, ultimately, revenues. The change that was supposed to enhance revenues often makes targets harder to achieve. As one client of ours shared recently, "Trying to get something accomplished across the siloes here requires full-on kamikaze warfare." In these conditions, urgency is tough to rationalize.

The second piece of context around the idea of urgency is that urgency is contextual. You should ask the question, "Urgent for whom?" Because, for most of the organization, one more change really may not even be noticed much; it's simply going to be survived. If you want to create urgency for a change, talk to the people who will be most affected by it and find out how urgent it is for them. If they are honest, they may tell you that in the scheme of things, the change isn't that important.

All of this said, there is a better way for organizations to create change. People don't automatically resist change; they resist change that is done *to* them, rather than *with* them. If you focus on a change that is meaningful to the organization's people and involve them in envisioning the future, you can worry less about creating urgency for change. When involved in defining the change, people usually become passionately involved in helping drive it forward.

> **When involved in defining the change, people usually become passionately involved in helping drive it forward.**

Building a Coalition to Drive and Support Change

One of the choice points you will face in laying the groundwork for visionary thinking is determining the participant list for the visioning process. Questions like, "how many people?" and "whom to include?" rise quickly to the surface. It's helpful to consider the use of some criteria to use in the selection of participants. We have noticed that most of our clients think too narrowly about who should participate. Think about how many areas may be touched by the possible changes, and who is involved in those areas. How can you include solid representation from those areas? Think beyond the borders of the company, about customers and clients of the organization, and see if you can include them, as well. Union leaders may be important as they have unique perspectives and input and can help sell the vision to their members. Human resources and talent leaders also often have keen insight into the company culture and add value.

Here are some examples of questions you might ask yourself in selecting your participants:

- Is this person an early adopter – someone who likes and is influential in driving change?

- Does this person need to be included, simply because if they are not, they will actively or passively block the change efforts?

- Do they represent a key group of constituents?

- Are their various points of view – in terms of work experience, nationality, etc. – relevant to the task at hand adequately represented?

- Does the group have enough people with strong credibility in the organization so that its decisions will be taken seriously by others?

- Does the group include enough formal and informal leaders to be able to drive the implementation of the vision?

We have a bias for wider rather than narrower inclusion. The bottom line is that you should think forward into the future and imagine who and how many people would be needed for successful change implementation. Be expansive in your thinking and remember that taking time to include more people upfront could very well be the most important decision that you make.

These are the key factors that we find influence the creation of the right conditions for change to occur. You and your team must:

- be able to learn how to use dialogue, at least to some extent, so that assumptions and beliefs can be openly explored;

- have a broadly representative group;

- understand the degree of urgency and relevance of the change from the team and employee perspective.

If the degree of urgency in the group is very low, you may be investing in a no-win initiative. In that case, consider aligning around a different opportunity. Applying visionary thinking around higher engagement or wellness goals, for example, have large ROIs and lends itself well to the whole-brain approach.

Clarifying Benefits of Creating a Shared Vision Around a Challenge

Discussing the benefits of a shared vision process is an important step in laying the groundwork.

Potential Benefits of Creating a Change Vision

- Provides an overarching framework for day-to-day decisions

- Creates high level of alignment

- Enhances a creative mind-set

- Inspires action

- Promotes pro-active attitudes

- Reduces the need for tight controls

- Stimulates learning

- Improves results

It's important that each team discusses its own aspirations and what it would like to see as the benefit of spending time and resources to create a shared vision. Use this very simple tool to help clarify the purpose and identify benefits to your team. It must be tailored to your situation.

Finally, take time to generate ideas for how the team might overcome these concerns.

In addition to identifying the purpose and desired benefits of creating a shared vision around a specific challenge, this exercise helps build commitment into the upcoming visioning process and ensure a smoother transition.

Invite the team to take a minute or two to relax. Explain that being relaxed increases the level of focus. Invite them to close their eyes, if they choose, and to imagine that it's six months (or whatever time perspective is desirable) from now.

The date is _____

A very successful process of creating a vision around the opportunity of _____ is now winding down. The vision that you and your team have created together is appealing, motivating, and realistic! And, today _____ (future date) you are already noticing how having this vision is positively affecting your priorities and decision making. Indeed, you and your team have good reason to celebrate. The benefits of this whole process of creating a shared vision are already becoming apparent. Today, you are delighted with the outcomes of the process and with the vision itself.

So . . .

- How are you, (your team, your function, external stakeholders) benefiting from the fact that you now have a shared vision around the opportunity of _____ ?

- What are you now more capable of doing, both as an individual leader and as a team?

Ask the members of the group to share the benefits they imagined in pairs or threes, and then in the group as a whole. After identifying and discussing the potential benefits, invite each person to share their concerns. Let each one note down all their concerns and prioritize the one or two they feel are most important. Invite the team to share whatever concerns they might have. Then, encourage the team to turn these concerns into opportunities.

Examples of concerns could be:	**Examples of opportunities could be:**
• We probably won't have time to implement something new!	• How might we ensure that we design enough implementation time into our vision action planning?
• It will be difficult to get the buy-in of people in other departments!	• How can we roll this out in such a way as to gain buy-in from those who are most crucial for implementation?
• We have no idea what the budget implications will be!	• In what ways might we avoid creating undesirable budgetary impacts?

Figure 7: Clarifying the Benefits of a Shared Visioning Approach

Clarifying the Benefits of a Shared Visioning Approach

Relaxation and Imagery Practice

In addition to learning dialogue skills and creating urgency for change, it's important that you become comfortable in leading relaxation and guided imagery exercises. Most groups need a structured way to transition to a more relaxed and fully present state of mind. Once relaxed, it's helpful to lead them through a couple of brief sessions in practicing visualization.[7] Afterwards, debrief the experience by asking people about their images and how comfortable they were. Most groups are quite enthusiastic about the imaging practice and are often eager to get going with the actual visioning process itself. Some general principles that will help you better understand the value of these practices and how to deliver them are:

· Take time to orient the group to the idea of guided imagery

Typically, some people will be more familiar and comfortable with guided imagery than others. Sharing information about the process and explaining the specific activities you will be using puts most people more at ease.

· Stress the importance of relaxation

Learning how to relax prior to visioning is a critical success factor. Most people and teams are not in an optimal and relaxed state of mind at the beginning of a session.

Taking the time to quiet racing minds and help people release tension helps everyone become more present and fully engaged with the visioning opportunity.

7　We have included examples of both relaxation and guided imagery scripts in the Appendix.

- Invite people to close their eyes

Guided imagery works best when people are willing to close their eyes during both the relaxation exercise and imaging practice. When our eyes are open, thousands of images flash on the retina and optical nerves, making it difficult for the brain to sort out the outer and inner images. However, if some people are uncomfortable with closing their eyes, have them practice imaging first with the eyes open. Most people become more comfortable with closing their eyes as they gain more experience with the visioning process.

- Provide opportunities to for people to experience their ability to image

Some people may be convinced that they have little imagination and cannot create mental images other than in their dreams or daydreams. Give these people the opportunity to experience their ability to respond to guided imagery. Suggest that they let images come in a completely non-judgmental way. Allow the images to flow and see where they take you.

- Remind people that there is no one right way to visualize

Some people say they see very clear, sharp images when they close their eyes; others find themselves just "thinking about" it or gaining a felt sense of the image. Remind them that we are all imagining the future all the time, we are just learning to do it in a more conscious and productive way.

Summary

We have spent some time helping you understand the groundwork for creating a shared vision. We've suggested some of the key areas that need to be discussed with any team that you want to facilitate in a visioning process. We discussed the importance of teaching your team dialogue skills, deciding who to include and how to monitor and build momentum. And in the Appendix, we have provided you with several imaging practice and relaxation exercises to get your team going in the right direction.

However, there is still a very important piece of work you need to do – design the script for desired future state scene, deciding which questions you will ask the group to envision responses to in that future state. This can be tricky, but when you get it right, the visioning process flows easily. Chapter Four provides a step-by-step approach to doing this.

Developing a Script for Envisioning Change

In this chapter, we will describe effective ways to facilitate change through creating a shared vision. As we discussed in Chapter One, we use guided imagery to increase utilization of the non-linear, intuitive and creative capabilities of the brain. In this process, after a brief period of relaxation and warm-up exercises, team members are guided to individually access their imagination and insight specifically in relation to the desired future state. Through guided imagery, rational, emotional and intuitive processes begin to work together. Nuances, context, images, feelings and insight about the future are identified in levels of detail not accessible in a typical planning or goal-setting process. This is the magic of a whole-brain approach – access to and leverage of a fuller breadth of cognitive capacity.

A well-written script is the foundation for helping a team visualize what they want to create. The script should be a carefully crafted narrative that provides just enough guidance about the future to be entirely relevant and relatable, while not intruding upon or limiting the creativity of the team. The script must successfully move the team forward in time to a desired future state that is appealing, motivating and attainable. It should pose meaningful questions that stimulate the flow of imagery and free the imagination. It should be easily understood by those who are envisioning the future.

These six steps are a good overview of the script-writing process. Let's walk through them in detail.

Decide Upon a Future Date When the Desired Future State Will Take Place

The key is to help the group members imagine they have arrived at a specified, successful point in the future – where everything they have wanted to create in relation to the challenge has been realized. When deciding upon a date, ensure that it is far enough into the future to allow for significant changes, yet close enough to motivate. It is the tension felt from comparing a mental image of a desired future with today's reality that fuels the vision. If a date is chosen that is too far into the future, there is too little tension and people lose interest in working towards it. The experience of imagining that they have arrived at a specific point in the future – that they are there, right now – unleashes a whole new set of innovative ideas. Somewhere between one and five years is often the right horizon into the future for change visions relating to most organizational challenges. However, 10 years is not uncommon when the aim is to envision a radical or large-scale change.

Select and Describe the Future Setting and Role

After deciding on the specific date to which they will fast-forward into the future, decide how best to stimulate the imagination of those participating in the vision exercise. Select a setting (in the future) and the specific role that everyone will play in that future setting. Collaboration with the client will ensure the most relevant scenes and roles. A setting in the future could be: an all-hands meeting in the same company in which they are working, where outstanding results from the change are being announced; an award ceremony where the company is getting an award in the area they are wanting to change in; or a setting where they are hovering above their future workplace and visualizing the positive changes that have occurred in the time that has passed. The possibility for settings are unlimited, if they are relevant and relatable to the team.

Figure 8: Being in a Different Role in the Future

It's also important for the script to define the role the participants will play in the future setting. The script can be built around the group members imagining themselves in a very different role than they are currently in, or they can continue to be in their existing roles but in the much more compelling setting of the desired future state. Here are some examples of what we mean by different roles:

Being in a Different Role in the Desired Future State

 **Journalist**

Imagine that you are a journalist for an industry relevant and respected magazine or a highly regarded newspaper or national or international magazine who, because of the favorable rumors, is asked to interview its leaders, employees, union leaders, stakeholders or customers. You listen to the comments from these stakeholders and write about the outstanding achievements of the organization (or function, department or project team, depending on the challenge).

 Professional Photographer or Videographer

Imagine that you are an experienced professional photographer asked by the editor of [choose an important industry relevant newspaper, magazine or publication] to take photos/snapshots/videos of the company and their accomplishment of [the desired future state]. As photographer, you walk through the company or visit the organization and observe interactions between people, systems, processes [or whatever is the focus for the change vision] and take photos of anything that illustrates key elements of the desired future state.

 TV or Radio Host

Imagine that your role as a TV or radio host is to interview some of the leaders in this company who have achieved amazing results in the past few years. Your job is to ask questions to find out what is going on in the company today, making it the key player in its industry or field.

Outside Observer or Witness

Imagine you are an outside observer and your role is simply to observe or witness the changes by walking through the facility or company, noting down what is going on in terms of process, systems, culture, productivity, safety, communication, etc.

 Customer or Key Stakeholder

Imagine your role is that of the company's future customer or key stakeholder, sharing why, today, you prefer to buy products or services from this organization. Talk about the kinds of advantages or benefits you experience, whether they be quality, personalized service or whatever the focus of the visioning is.

 Consultant in a Leading Consultancy Firm

Imagine your role is that of a consultant to this company. In this future state, you are witness to a whole host of behaviors, values, processes, priorities or other differentiators that are making this company incredibly successful. Explore these in detail, identifying them one by one.

 Manager in a Competitor Company

Imagine your role is that of a leader in a company that competes with your actual company. In this desired future state, as the competitor, you are struggling to compete with this company. You talk with your other colleagues about the products or services, operating procedures, values, customer behaviors or whatever you are observing that is positively differentiating this company and making it tough to compete with.

Being Yourself in the Desired Future State

Figure 9: Being Yourself in the Future

The second approach to role identification is to allow the members of the group to continue being themselves, but at a specific date in the future (and thereby, the corresponding number of years older depending on the time frame) and envision the positive outcomes they have achieved.

Being Invited to Be the Keynote Speaker at a Conference

Imagine you are standing in front of an audience at a national or international conference, showing slides and hearing yourself speak about the positive outcomes and surprising impacts of the challenge or opportunity that your team addressed.

Being Invited to Be an Observer

Imagine you are observing what's going on in the organization from a new perspective. For example, standing on the roof and looking down through a large hole, or looking in through a large window where you can observe the layout, logistics, production flow, or machinery of a newly designed facility.

Reading a Feature Article in a Prestigious Magazine, Newspaper or Blog

Imagine a feature article describing your organization's success. What are the headlines? What is the buzz about your company?

Attending a Prestigious National or International Conference – Give It an Appropriate Name

Imagine walking into a large conference room, finding a seat and listening with pride to a speaker announcing an award, or sharing the outstanding accomplishments of the group that has successfully addressed the challenge.

Walking Slowly Through a Specific Space

Imagine walking slowly through a specific space, for example, a reception area, offices, meeting rooms, cafeteria, etc. and noticing what it is about the way it is designed, how it functions or how interactions are happening between employees and/or customers that makes it productive and appealing.

Meeting With Various Company Stakeholders

Imagine yourself in a meeting with various stakeholders posing questions to them about how things are going at the company in regards to this new future state and listening to their responses.

Flying in a Balloon or Traveling in a Car, Bus or Train

Imagine traveling through a landscape, town or harbor during one or more seasons of the year.

Notice and appreciate what is taking place beneath you or what you observe around you as it relates to the desired future state.

These are just a few approaches to selecting roles for the visioning process. Keep in mind that you need to:

- Determine how far into the future you want to lead the group

- Identify the kind of setting that will work best for envisioning your particular challenge

- Select a specific role that participants/teams will play in the future state.

Select and Formulate Questions

When we invite people to mentally move into the future and imagine a changed and desired future state, we ask the group to respond to questions that free their imagination and stimulate relevant images of new possibilities. There are so many options to choose from in terms of formulating the right questions for any given visioning opportunity! The question-formulation stage is important and worth taking some time over. Discuss the kinds of questions you are thinking about asking with a few key stakeholders, both to get input on their relevance, and also to encourage buy-in ahead of time.

Questions That Seem to Function Best are Questions That:

▶ Are open-ended and naturally stimulate images that are relevant to the future state of the challenge or focus

▶ Are phrased in the present tense, as if the future state already exists (e.g., What are we being recognized for? What differences are our efforts making?)

▶ Describe a future state that is very attractve to the client

▶ Reflect values and positive emotions (e.g. What are you most proud of? What are your top three accomplishments or big wins?)

It is equally important to avoid posing questions that:

- demand "yes" or "no" responses;

- stimulate images that lead the mind back to the past and "how we got here" or "why we did what we did".

Some consultants who facilitate visionary thinking have a standard set of questions they believe are equally effective regardless of the type of organization. We have not found this to be so. When facilitating visionary thinking where the focus can be any one of many different challenges, so the key is not only to design a script tailored to the specific situation, but also to identify the three or four questions that are the most relevant and are in harmony with the setting of the script.

Questions can have to do with almost any aspect of the business – values, specific areas of performance, competencies, customers, technological or organizational innovations, behaviors, environment, cultural attributes or collaboration. The client or leader should lead the way in identifying the specific areas of emphasis for the visioning, which are then reinforced through the specific questions that are asked in the session.

Below are examples of questions we have used on different occasions. They are by no means exhaustive. They are intended to trigger ideas for questions that can be formulated in a way to make them more relevant to the challenge that is in focus. We have used the we/us voice in our questions below, but voice can be adapted depending on the role the client has been given in the script. Before reading through these questions, you might allow yourself to imagine that it is two years from today's date.

Questions Relating to Our Business, Role and Values

- What difference are our efforts making?

- What contributions is our organization making to society?

- What makes us distinctive and unique?

- What are we being recognized for?

- What are we most proud of?

- How is our organization (group/department/company) different from others in the same industry?

- How are we helping other departments (functions/plants/units) in our organization become more successful?

- What are our stakeholders (e.g., owners, local community, environmental organizations, etc.) saying about us?

- How is [key value] manifesting in our interactions with one another, customers, the local community, etc.?

- What is meaningful about our work?

- What are we doing today to take care of the environment?

- What practices or group norms are making our organization such an attractive workplace?

- What explains the high degree of enthusiasm and commitment evident in our organization today?

- What contribution is our function making to the organization?

Questions Relating to Our Products, Services and Customers

- What are our core products?

- What services do we provide?

- Who are our internal customers?

- Who are our external customers?

- What characterizes our products/services?

- What are we doing to develop/create new products?

- What is it about our services that customers are willing to pay for?

- What are we doing today that is attracting new customers?

- What added value are our customers experiencing?

- What are the three most noteworthy things our customers/suppliers say about our company?

- What do our customers value most about our products?

- How do we go about successfully identifying our customers' needs?

- What new ways are we marketing our products and services today?

- What is it that our customers value most about our products/services?

- Why are our customers choosing/demanding our products/services?

Questions Relating to Leadership/Employee Relationships

- What are the hallmarks of our leadership today?

- What are the qualities that characterize our leadership team?

- What are the tasks we as a leadership team give most priority to today?

- What makes us proud of our leadership team?

- What enables employees to receive the information they need?

- What are we doing that inspires people to seek employment with us?

- What is leadership doing that stimulates creative thinking throughout the organization?

- What are employees saying about why they are excited about working here?

- How are teams working with one another across silos? What is new and different?

- Why is it working so well?

- What are the specific structures and practices that are making this new level of collaboration so successful?

Once you have formulated several questions, you need to think through how you will fast forward the team into the desired future setting.

Scripts for Fast Forwarding to the Future

Sometimes it is sufficient to just invite a group to close their eyes, take some long slow depth breaths, let go of any tension they feel, and then imagine that the date is one year from today's date (or whatever length of time you have chosen). Often, however, it is useful to help a group mentally move into the future. Once you have helped the group achieve a relaxed state of mind, use a Fast Forward script. In Appendix 3, we offer two examples of how to do this as well as a third further on in this chapter. We encourage you to customize these so that they work for your group.

Tips for Presenting the Scene

As you lead a group through the visioning process, speak in a slow, relaxed and deliberate manner. The quality of your voice is as important as the words you use. Avoid speaking constantly as that can pull awareness away from each person's internal experience. This will support the group in maintaining a focus on their mental images. As much as possible, you, too need to experience everything you say in the script. A good way to prepare for this part of the process is to record yourself reading the script and experience it as a participant. Ask yourself if you are taking enough pauses throughout the script, if you sound believable to yourself, and if your script holds together and leads you into the future in a powerful and relevant manner?

Begin the visualization with a phrase like the one below:

"As we move into this visualization, I'd like you to keep your attention on the sound of my voice and on what I am saying. We are going to move together into the future in a way that will enhance your ability to conjure images. [Pause] I am going to give you suggestions and instructions. As much as possible, visualize what you hear in a clear, vivid and detailed way.

Try to put yourself within the scene that is described as completely as you can."

Pay close attention to how the group is responding to the visioning process. Some people will naturally adapt to it more quickly than others. Try not to take fidgeting or other behaviors as a sign that they don't want to participate. They may just be finding it difficult to focus. You may be able to gently provide additional guidance to help them, such as: *"If you find it hard to focus, try taking a deep breath and bringing your mind back to the visioning process."*

Before you move into the actual script for the visioning, be sure to lead one of the imagery practice exercises included in the Appendix. Then you can segue into a relaxation exercise, also included in the Appendix. Note that you will move directly from the relaxation exercise into the visioning script without debriefing or asking people to open their eyes. This ensures that the team can stay in a quiet, creative mindset for the visioning.

It's very important to adopt an appreciative mindset throughout the process. This means you actively validate and appreciate everyone's unique experiences. Someone may believe that they are terrible at imaging and that they didn't see anything. It's important for you to reframe this for them as a learning experience and reassure them it will get easier with practice. As Andrew Schwartz says in his book, *Guided Imagery for Groups*, "There is no one right way to read relaxation and guided imagery scripts. There is one essential guideline for reading: take your time. Remember that your listeners do not know what is coming. They need time for the mental images to form and unfold. They need time to explore and sense. They need time to make transitions."[8]

> **It's very important to adopt an appreciative mindset throughout the process. This means you actively validate and appreciate everyone's unique experiences.**

---

8 Schwartz, Andrew E. Guided Imagery for Groups. Duluth, MN: Whole Person Associates, Inc., 1995, pg 14.

Transitioning to Individual Reflection

After completing the script, move into an individual reflection process that allows each person to quietly review and think more about their vision. We'll discuss this more in Chapter Five, so suffice to say, keep people in a meditative state while you help move them into an individual reflection exercise.

We have completed all the steps of the script writing process. Now let's look at a case study that illustrates the process in its entirety. We have also included some participant feedback at the end of the study so you can gauge the impact of the process.

A Case Study: Envisioning the Future of Sustainable Food Systems

Background

The Department of Plant Sciences at the Norwegian University of Life Sciences offers a M.Sc. in Agroecology. Agroecology is a cross-disciplinary, action-oriented field of study that aims to provide a holistic understanding of the entire food system encompassing its social, economic, environmental and institutional dimensions.

An integral part of the program is to help students better understand the complex web in which farm and food systems are embedded, and to aid them in becoming effective facilitators of change. To enable students to take on this role as change agents, they need to learn and practice certain competencies – competencies that will be essential throughout their academic and field studies, thesis research and in future professional positions. These include skills in **observation, participation, dialogue** and **visionary thinking**. Embedded in each of these skills is an additional competency – the ability **to reflect** on one's own experience. The parts of the program that focus on dialogue and visionary thinking were designed and introduced by Marjorie Parker and have been successfully in use for over 20 years.[9]

Knowledge and skill training in all these competencies are part of the first semester of the M.Sc. Program entitled *Action Learning in Farming and Food Systems*. The students come from different countries and cultural backgrounds and the program is run in English. At the beginning of the course, students are divided into project teams of 4-5 each. Each team is assigned a specific municipality in Norway, and over the course of several weeks, they prepare to carry out a case study in their area. As an aid to clarifying the current situation within their municipality, each team creates what's called a "rich picture" in which complex situations are represented in a large diagram with pictures and symbols. The principle behind rich pictures is that drawing detailed representations of problematic situations can be a tool to organize thoughts, better understand what is going on in the system, and identify root problems.

After the rich picture experience, students have a two-day introduction to visionary thinking. To experience their own ability to create images, they are led through a relaxation exercise followed by imagery practice. Examples of the imagery practice used is in the Appendix, and we will start with an example of a relaxation exercise given to the students.

Getting Started by Relaxing

The following is a practical example of the relaxation exercise given to students:

"In this exercise, you can participate in any way you feel is best for you. If you want to participate in the exercise by following my instructions, that's great. If you would rather be an observer to the exercise, and just see

---

9 In competition with other institutions of higher learning in Norway, the Department of Plant Sciences was recently presented with the prestigious Education Quality Award (one million NOK) by the Minister of Education for its innovative M.Sc. in Agroecology program. The purpose of the Education Quality Award is to reward excellence in education in Norwegian higher education and to stimulate institutions and academic communities to work systematically on refining the quality of their programs.

what it is all about, that is quite okay too. Research has shown that we can more easily bring forth our mental images when we are in a relaxed state. Therefore, I am going to read aloud a simple relaxation exercise for you. Some of you have perhaps experienced this, or similar ones, previously. You'll find this is a great exercise anytime you want to increase your level of focus, calm your nervous system or connect with a quieter place inside. So, sit as comfortably as you can and close your eyes. Do not cross your legs or arms.

"To warm up, we are going to spend a few minutes just relaxing. Try to follow my counting instructions, but you should never strain or struggle to hold your breath. If it feels difficult at any point, or if you feel dizzy, simply lessen the amount of time you inhale, hold and exhale.

"Let's start by getting comfortable. Rub your hands together to create some heat, then press your hands to your face and give yourself a little face rub."

[Pause.]

"Now, gently close your eyes or fix your gaze on something directly in front of you. Become aware of your breathing. I'm going to slowly guide you on a journey where you can gradually relax all the parts of your body.

"Let's begin with your feet. Squeeze your toes a few times and become aware of the energy that flows into them as you do that simple movement. Take a deep breath and sigh out any tension in your feet. Then become aware of your calves. Tighten your calf muscles and release them several times, feeling the flow of energy increase to your lower legs. Then become aware of your thighs. Tighten and then release those muscles, feeling the increase of energy flowing through them.

"Now notice your buttock muscles, feel your sitz bones pressing into the chair. Become aware of your pelvis and groin, and take some deep breaths into this area of the body, just noticing the flow of energy that is created by your breath.

"Move your awareness up to your belly, take some deep breaths way down into the belly area. Sigh out any tension you may be holding and bring awareness to the warmth that is created as you focus there. Now bring your awareness up to your chest, your heart, your lungs, allowing your breath to deepen even further. Try to empty your lungs with each exhalation.

"If you feel dizzy just return to normal breathing, but try to really focus here, feeling the energy relax, energize and heal your entire torso. Now bring your awareness to your shoulders and arms, sending the breath all the way down your arms to your fingertips. Stay there and breathe, allow the breath to bring you back to the sensations in your body, leaving the mental chatter behind. Finally, bring your attention up through your neck through the back of your head, across the crown of the head and then down into the forehead, eyes, ears, nose, cheeks and mouth. Keep breathing there until you can feel a gentle flow of energy relaxing your brain, your face, your neck and your throat."

The students are now invited to imagine being ten years in the future and envisioning the situation in the municipality where they, as students, successfully contributed to the development of urban agriculture and alternative food networks. They are invited to envision what is different today (ten years in the future) and how various stakeholders are benefiting from this change.

Mentally Moving into the Future

"Now, I am going to ask you to imagine that you can travel into the future. I'd like you to imagine that you are going to fast-forward to ten years from today, to the year 2027. To make it easier for you to mentally experience transitioning to the year 2027, I invite you to imagine that you have your own unique vehicle to achieve your transportation to the future. You might have an affinity for magic carpets and if so, take a minute or two to imagine the patterns, colors and comfort of your personal carpet. Now is your perfect opportunity to take a ride. Or, maybe you have always had a secret desire to be the pilot of a hot air balloon. If so, picture the color or pattern of your balloon, remembering that it can be a big or small as you want it to.

"Take a few seconds now to create an image of the vehicle you think it would be most exciting to travel into the future with. [Pause.] Now, I would like you to see yourself standing on the lawn outside of this building. Feel the air. Notice the color of the leaves. Notice whether it's sunny or cloudy. Now, notice that your own unique vehicle is also on the lawn, only a few meters away from you. Take a careful look at it. Walk around and admire it."

[Pause.]

"Now, climb into it or on it. Adjust your seating, give it the proper command, cast off the rope, or turn on the ignition and make yourself as comfortable as possible. Prepare for takeoff.

"Allow your vehicle to slowly and gently lift you off the ground. A little bit higher, and still little higher. So high that you notice, when you look down, you can see the rooftops of the buildings below. Notice the fields on the other side of the road and how they look this time of year.

"Be aware that your vehicle is now heading in westerly direction . . . that you are now travelling over and away from the university campus. You are heading west.

"Over the rolling plain of wheat, above the forest and river valleys. Perhaps by now you are over the mountains . . . the glaciers and plateau of Hardangervidda mountain range . . . notice their amazing beauty and the early snow.

"Now, looking down over the countryside, you find you are coming closer to the fjords of western Norway. Off in the distance, on the south-west coast, you see a glimpse of Stavanger.

"Notice now that your vehicle is beginning to move more slowly and that you are gradually beginning to float downwards, ever so gently. The time has come for you to prepare to land. Allow yourself now to easily and slowly go in for landing on a beautiful green field."

Description of Future Scene

"Now that you have landed safely . . . take a look around you. Today is November 17, 2027.

You are 10 years older! And undoubtedly 10 years wiser!

"About 20 meters off to your right, you see a large building. It appears to be a beautiful conference center. Looking at it from the outside, what is it that impresses you?

"Now, feel yourself walking towards the main entrance to that building. Notice the large sign over the entrance. It says, '**Sustainable Norway: Urban Agriculture and Alternative Food Networks**.'

"Enter the building and walk towards the exhibition hall. In front of the exhibition hall, you see a sign bearing the words, '**Success stories from the Norwegian Spaces of Hope Project**.'

"Standing on the podium is the conference leader. Hear him saying in a loud clear voice:

'Welcome! Today we are proud to announce that Urban Agriculture and alternative food networks have been established in three major municipalities in Norway. All three municipalities are receiving recognition nationally and internationally for their amazing achievements. Connections between farmers and consumers have multiplied. In newspapers, blogs and other media we read glowing accounts about how people in the municipalities are involved in urban agricultural activities and promoting the use of organic food. An outstanding achievement!

'What's behind all of this? Without doubt, it has grown due to the successful collaboration between the project team and local stakeholders – farmers, processors, distributors and consumer groups, as well as with governmental institutions and environmental organizations in the municipality.

'We are fortunate to have here with us the local project leader, who is willing to share what is going on in the municipality and the reasons why it is a model for the rest of the country in advancing sustainable food systems and programs.

You must feel very proud about having made such a difference in your municipality. Knowing how much is going on today in your municipality regarding urban agriculture and alternative food networks, tell us what you are most proud of?'

"Just listen quietly to how you respond. You do not need to censor anything. [Pause.]

'In what specific ways are the inhabitants in the municipality benefiting from this new situation? [Pause.] And the farmers in the region, how are they benefiting?'

"Again, listen to how you respond.

[Pause.]

'What else do you see happening in this municipality that makes it a model for the rest of the country with regard to advancing sustainable food systems?'

[Pause.]

'Many thanks for your willingness to be with us today and share your insights.'

"Allow yourself to feel pride in having been asked to share what is going on in the municipality where you and your team have made such an enormous and positive impact. Listen to the audience applauding. [Pause.]

"Now see yourself walking slowly out of the exhibition area, out of the conference center, and out into the open air.

"On the lawn, not far from the conference building, is a white painted bench. See yourself sitting down on the bench. I will now ask you to open your eyes. Remain silent and please do not speak with your neighbor. You will now have time to note your responses to the questions posed by the conference leader."

[Write questions on whiteboard or flipchart so the participants can look in case they have forgotten.]

"Remember – it is still November 17, 2027, and your responses are describing the achievements that are now manifesting in the year 2027. Write your responses in the present tense. If, in addition to words, it feels easier to illustrate your responses by making a drawing or sketch, feel free to do so. There are crayons on the table. Feel free to use your non-dominant hand to make the drawing. It does not matter if the drawings are simple or rough sketches. You have plenty of time to do this. If you complete the writing/drawing before the others, remain in your chair and be completely quiet."

Participants then share their responses and/or drawing in groups of four and follow the process for refining their visions as described in Chapter Five.

Participant Feedback on the Visionary Process of the Program[10]

The use of dialogue and shared visioning has become a very successful part of the Agroecology program. In addition to envisioning the outcomes

10 This unique M.Sc. program has been written about in many articles. The following reference

of their casework, the students also envision the type of collaboration within their project team needed to ensure they achieve their desired outcomes. As part of the case work, the students hold public workshops and take on the role of facilitator, helping the municipality's stakeholders create their own shared visions and collectively come up with action plans for stimulating the development of urban agriculture and alternative food networks. Back on the university campus, each project team prepares an in-depth stakeholder document for the farmers, distributors, policy-makers and other stakeholders in their assigned municipality. As preparation for writing this, they also create shared visions of a user-friendly, inspiring, well-structured document.

We include here a few examples of how the students experience applying visionary thinking as part of their graduate program.

"The visioning seminar was the main factor making this program very different from all the previous courses I have taken. Never had I approached a situation from the perspective of what I wanted to create in the future. All other work had considered the current situation and then attempted to solve the problems to make the system better. The visioning seminar was particularly appropriate for a situation, which is hard to divide into its smaller parts. The emergent properties of a food system are simply too complex to reduce into its individual parts. Visioning allowed us to look at the whole system without becoming bogged down in unimportant details."

Student from USA

---

provides more information: Francis, C., E. Østergaard, A.M. Nicolaysen, T.A. Breland, G. Lieblein, and S. Morse. 2016. Learning through Involvement and Reflection in Agroecology. In: Mendez, VE, C.M. Bacon, R. Cohen & S.R. Gliessman (eds) Agroecology: a transdisciplinary, participatory and action-oriented approach. CRC Press Advances in Agroecology Series. 73 – 99.

"*Before the visionary thinking seminar, we had little direction. We felt like we were treading water but not getting anywhere with our work. While we were far from strongly confident after the seminar, we felt we had much better material to work with afterwards.*"

Student from USA

"*As part of our work (during our case study) we worked with visioning as a tool. Through our work with visioning and sensing, the strength of the feedback received from the recipients of our work with the vision made me think. On one side, we felt much empowered to work with visioning – the liberating and creative feeling of not being stuck in the web of complex reality. On the other side, we felt the positive feedback from those who listened to the results of our work. It has made me think a lot about how visioning can be a way to empower and engage people in change. To work with the task to bring people together and 'let them loose' on their ideas for the future – seems like a fabulous way to bring ownership and desire to change. This will be one of the things to bring on into my future studies and work.*"

Student from Iceland

"*Visioning as a tool was completely new to me. In the beginning, I felt quite critical about it. It was nice to use in a class of open-minded students, but it felt quite strange to use it with people who had never heard of it before. For me, it helped not to think about the whole process too much, but to focus on the aims and the benefits. And it is a brilliant way to create a goal for yourself or a shared one together. Not emphasizing current problems or limitation really helps to get to the core and to be creative. You don't want to solve one or two problems; you want the whole situation to move to a higher level and a better situation. I think his makes it an ideal tool to use in messy situations."*

Student from Holland

You now have an overview of how to create the future roles and scene, identify the best questions, warm up the group and help them envision a desired future state using a whole-brain approach. Without a doubt, this is the most difficult part of the process, but once you have done it a few times, you will find it begins to flow more intuitively. In the next chapter, we will explore the steps for moving from many individual visions to the creation of a shared vision.

Chapter Five

From Individual to Shared Vision

"The more you talk to people and listen to them, the clearer your vision will become. Whenever a person talks, they have a chance to hear their thoughts out loud. They get clearer on what they are trying to say. After listening to people respond to your ideas, your vision will probably change somewhat. You may want to incorporate some of their thinking into your own."

Marya Axner, Community Toolbox

At this point in the process, you will have successfully conducted the first visioning session and are about to invite your group to open their eyes – but now what? There are some best practices to observe in the process of ensuring that these newly born visions survive the transition back to current day. Not only that, you will need a way to help move the group from numerous individual visions to one shared vision. The following four steps provide an effective transition process. We will explore each in more depth.

A Four-Step Process

Individual Reflection

Participants need some time to reflect on and clarify their individual vision so that they become more concrete and memorable. This often segues into writing or drawing.

Small Group Sharing: Deep Listening

Participants get into small groups where people provide appreciative listening to each other's visions.

Group Dialogue: Finding Common Themes

The group works together to identify the common themes and key points of alignment.

Group Discussion: Establishing Criteria/Aligning Around the Shared Vision

The group begins to use a more convergent thinking process, narrowing the options and starting to select the most important elements of the shared vision.

1. Individual reflection

A challenge that crops up in the immediate aftermath of a visioning experience is, *how can each participant stay connected to their individual visions long enough to convey them to the other participants with the same degree of vividness and enthusiasm as they experienced during the guided imagery exercise?* We have yet to see anyone who doesn't feel excited by his or her individual vision. The experience of moving into the future and envisioning the desired outcome of an important challenge is inevitably uplifting.

Create a flipchart that has the 3-4 questions from the script that you read during the guided imagery. Or, hand out the questions to each participant prior to this session. Once you have asked them to focus on the questions, remain silent so that they can give all their attention to the images they came up with. It's also helpful to remind them that people experience vision in many different ways. If they did not see any pictures, that is perfectly okay. Ask them to focus on whatever came up in response to the questions. You will need to coach the group to remain silent during this section so that they can focus internally.

Invite them to open their eyes, pick up a piece of paper and pen and write at the top of the page, "Today is . . ." and then the date and year in the future tense. This reminds them to write as if the future is now. Ask them to describe on paper, in as much detail as they can, the images they envisioned. You can also invite them to sketch or draw pictures or symbols of the images that were meaningful to them. Give them 15-20 minutes to do this and then ask them to put a star next to those ideas or images that are most central to their experience. By following a process like this, you ensure that each person has a stronger connection to their individual visions and something that feels important to them to share in the next phase of the process.

2. Small group sharing: deep listening

The transition from individual to small-group sharing is a delicate one. It requires careful facilitation so that people don't lose track of their individual visions. We have experimented with a variety of ways to create shared vision, and central to all of them is encouraging participants to be fully present in the *desired future state* when they begin to share what they experienced in the visualization.

It can be helpful to present some ground rules, for example you can suggest that a symbolic red card will be given to anyone who:

- Brings the discussion back to today's problems

- Begins to focus on the difficulties or barriers to achieving their own or their partner's visions

- Underestimates their own or others' abilities to realize the vision

- Gets hung up on how this is all going to happen

Once you have covered the ground rules, invite them to get into small groups to share the descriptions or images that they starred. Instruct them to share their visions in the present, as if the future they created in their minds already exists. For example: "It's 2026 and what is giving our customers added value is . . ." or "The way we are marketing our products today is . . ."

When one person shares, the others should simply listen and appreciate the images and descriptions. The idea is to make sure that each person's images are fully heard. Give them about 20-30 minutes for this small group sharing exercise. Be sure to walk around the room and gently correct people's language if they are straying into today's time frame or focusing on how to make changes. You will also want to make sure that everyone is getting a chance to share his or her vision and that one or two people aren't dominating the group.

3. Group dialogue: finding common themes

As the small groups complete their sharing process, invite them to come back together as the whole group. You'll need to reinforce the ground rules once again. Explain that the purpose of this next section is to explore the common themes that arose in the small groups. Ask each small group to share 3-4 elements of what they envisioned with the whole group. Write these on a flipchart or in a drawing. Ask some of those listening to share something they like about what they are hearing.

Remember that, while people usually feel excited about sharing their visions, they may also feel rather vulnerable when sharing them aloud. As we have mentioned previously, visions demand a leap of faith and imagination. They often contain innovative ideas that have never been thought of before; sharing them may feel risky. Most people have experienced having their new ideas shot down. Because of the natural tendency to look for faults or weaknesses in other peoples' ideas, it's extremely important that participants are asked to listen to one another's visions with an open mind and appreciative mindset.

> **Because of the natural tendency to look for faults or weaknesses in other peoples' ideas, it's extremely important that participants are asked to listen to one another's visions with an open mind and appreciative mindset.**

It can help if, as they listen, they ask themselves:

- What I find most appealing is . . .

- The three most positive aspects of this vision are . . .

- What would be interesting to take a step further is . . .

When all the groups have reported in, invite the whole group to identify the most common themes. Write these themes in words and/or drawings on a flip chart or whiteboard and invite the group to talk about them, focusing first on their responses to the three questions above.

As you identify themes, begin to link them together, where appropriate. If you have someone skilled in on-the-spot graphic depiction, that is extremely effective. However, even someone not so skilled can, with constructive help and input from the group, create pictures, symbols and words that depict common themes and illustrate the connections between them. Having some kind of visual representation that everyone in the group can see is always useful.

Take time to help the group work towards a shared understanding of each theme by clarifying the underlying assumptions of each one. This helps to move the group towards a shared vision. It also builds the team's level of ownership and commitment to implementing the vision.

4. Group discussion: establishing criteria/aligning around the shared vision

Once the group has identified the common themes from their visions, it's useful to generate criteria for evaluating which of the themes to include in the shared vision. After creating a list of possible criteria, help them select the ones they feel are the most important. You can use voting, if need be, but often the group is able to come to a consensus without that. Ask the team to evaluate the various aspects of the vision against the final criteria. Using a rating system like 1-5 or "red, yellow, green" helps the group test their vision against the criteria. We have found that 6-7 final criteria usually work well.

Additional criteria may have to do with time frames, costs involved, groups affected, tangibles (like materials or equipment needed), or moral or legal implications. Once the group has agreed upon the common themes or key elements of the vision, it may need refining.

As a final test, you might want the group to check whether the vision meets some overall general criteria by asking:

Does Our Vision . . .

- align with our values and those of the organization?

- depict a change that is lofty and challenging?

- make sense in the marketplace?

- feel genuine and authentic?

Or Will Our Vision . . .

- be perceived as compelling by those who will be affected by it?

- evoke meaningful images in the minds of others?

- be motivational even in hard times?

- be achievable within the chosen time frame?

This process supports the group in modifying and refining the vision, identifying something that has been missing or expanding on something important. Often, there is a need for a deeper shared understanding of what some of the words or images mean. At the end of this process, the shared vision should feel even stronger, more compelling, realistic and engaging. Helping a group move from individual visions to shared vision is incredibly important and takes time. There is a power that comes from alignment around a shared vision that is largely untapped in today's organizations. You can feel the energy of that alignment and it provides a great deal of force in overcoming inertia, resistance to change and the 'not invented here' syndrome.

In one of our largest projects, 1700 employees participated in a revitalization effort using visionary thinking. Participants spanned all levels of the organization and included factory workers, union leaders, executives and line staff. The leaders were surprised to witness the extent to which their employees shared insightful and innovative ideas for positive change. Leaders were even more surprised to see employees whom they previously would have characterized as negative or passive, offering radically new and constructive solutions to many of the organization's critical challenges.

The visions, expressed in songs and drawings as well as through written word, demonstrated employees' convictions about how best to relate to customers, suppliers, local communities, and the environment. They included descriptions of technical excellence, leadership, information flows, and union and management cooperation. It was a moving and humbling experience to witness this demonstration of the employee's deep commitment to making a better company. Later in the process, the employees generated criteria and selected those aspects they felt were the keys to a lofty, achievable and motivating vision for the company as a whole, their business unit and their department.

Chapter Six, Making Shared Visions Real, will help you direct the group towards the next steps towards achieving the vision. It includes a number of tools for communicating the vision, gaining acceptance for it, and catalyzing the organizational resources necessary for bringing it to life.

Making the Vision Real

"The real power of a vision is unleashed only when most of those involved in an enterprise or activity have common understanding of its goals and direction. That shared sense of a desirable future can help motivate and coordinate the kinds of actions that create transformations."

J. Kotter

At this point in the process, a lot has been accomplished. A shared vision has been articulated and there is a growing alignment and emotional engagement with it – in short, momentum is building. In this chapter, we'll explore how you can harness that energy and help the team move towards implementation planning, without losing the alignment, connection and clarity of the vision. We'll also explore that all-important aspect of implementation: communicating the vision to the broader organization.

The title of this chapter, "Making the Vision Real," is a somewhat contradictory expression. Once a team has created a powerful mental image of a desired future state, in a way, it is already real. Our images of the future exist in the present within our minds. If these images are aligned with our values, stir within us a sense of purpose, and make sense in the market place, then they will engage both our emotions and our intellect and create within us an urge to act. But, there is a big difference between a vision that lives in people's minds and one that has been translated into every day organizational life, influencing and impacting people well beyond the team or group that created the vision. Getting change to take root, to manifest fully, to come to life – these are the really tough parts of change initiatives.

Daniel Kim, systems thinker, author, and co-founder of the MIT Organization Learning Center, explains, "Many organizations that catch the vision 'fever' believe the job is finished once a small group of top managers produce a vision statement and announce it to the rest of the organization. Expecting that the vision, in and of itself, will produce transformation, the initial group often disregards the importance of the process that brought about the commitment. When misinterpreted in this way, vision becomes a thing that people are expected to buy into, rather than a lively process of sharing what we most care about in a way that creates enthusiasm and shared commitment."[11]

Understanding Levers for Change

Almost everyone is familiar with the dismal statistics on failed organizational change efforts – somewhere between 70% and 95%. And the culprit for these failures is typically attributed to people's 'resistance to change'. Let's dig into this idea more fully as it represents some popular assumptions about change that often derail change initiatives.

Kim explores the idea of these change-resistant people, stating, "As organizations undertake change efforts, much discussion and effort is usually devoted to dealing with people who are resistant to change. How do we convince them to go along with the plan? What incentives can we use to entice them to buy in? Rather than spending time formulating strategies to deal with these 'unchangeable' people, we should step back and ask ourselves, do they really exist? When invited to participate in creating something they truly care about, people are usually more than willing to change – and sometimes they are even impatient with the larger

11 Kim, Daniel. "The vision deployment matrix – a framework for large scale change". *The Systems Thinker*, accessed June 2017. https://thesystemsthinker.com/vision-deployment-matrix-aframework-for-large-scale-change/

organization's inability to move fast enough toward the goal. Most people do not resist change; they resist being changed when it is imposed from the outside."[12]

Perhaps we need to stop attributing people's unwillingness to adopt change solely on their bad attitudes and consider ways to include a wider range of people in meaningful exploration, dialogue and visioning about the future. Realistically, what other choice is there? It should be clear by now that mechanical change management initiatives in which people are 'engineered' through the change process without any meaningful engagement often waste significant amounts of time and money without yielding much in the way of results.

> **Perhaps we need to stop attributing people's unwillingness to adopt change solely on their bad attitudes and consider ways to include a wider range of people in meaningful exploration, dialogue and visioning about the future.**

In the shared visioning approach, the implementation-planning phase in the change process becomes a learning process in which perspectives must continually shift between the shared vision and the immediate actions that are needed to reach it.

If a shared visioning process has been successful, in the sense that employees have created, shared and agreed upon which mental images of the desired future state they are willing to commit to, then typically people:

- start living the vision immediately through their behaviors, attitudes and conversations;

- start sharing ideas for action steps that can move them in the direction of their vision.

There is no one right way to implement a shared vision. There are only more and less successful actions, all of which provide opportunities for

12 Ibid

learning. As one action step nears completion, new ideas for action are created in people's minds, assuming they are keeping the vision alive. In an effective whole-brain visioning approach, employees do not need to be told of the necessity of becoming change-oriented, they are continually changing and creating change around them.

The following example[13] illustrates the returns on a successfully implemented change vision.

Envisioning Health

As part of a large-scale revitalization process in a Norwegian company, all the employees (leaders and managers, union leaders, and all levels of staff) were introduced to visionary thinking using guided imagery. They were asked to envision themselves five years ahead in time observing what was going on in the factory when they were taking care of their own and each other's health. The visions were shared and inspired an enormous amount of creativity.

As a step in making the visions real, a team consisting of representatives from the company fitness club, the company health services, information department and cafeteria was established. Groups of employees in various parts of the company worked together to improve their diets, reduce weight, quit smoking and improve their physical well-being overall.

At the onset of this program, the company had an accident rate of 14 per million working hours. Three years later, the accident rate had been reduced by 50% to seven per million working hours. Over the three years, absenteeism was also reduced by about 50% from 6.47% to 3.5%. The Safety Inspector reasoned that the positive decline in the accident rate and absenteeism was because of participation and self-responsibility.

"We're not preoccupied with fixed goals; we recognize that it's all about a continual process of improving ourselves," a worker in the Reduction

13 Parker, Marjorie. Sammen om visjoner-Et pionerarbeid om nytenkning i praksis.Oslo: Hjemmets bokforlag AS, 1992.

plant shared. "We now show that we care for each other. To point out a mistake isn't regarded as something negative, but more as a step to prevent accidents. Everyone is their own safety inspector."

The visioning approach invited full participation, empowerment and led to a larger group of employees taking responsibility for their own health and safety. Companies that are serious about employee safety[14] and wellness may benefit from a shared visioning approach as an alternative to traditional goal setting. As we have commented previously, setting safety or wellness goals is much less effective than inviting people to envision how they could take better care of their own and one another's health. It inspires creativity, empowerment, commitment and action.

Kim provides further insight into the challenges of making the vision real: "In between vision and current reality lies an enormous 'chasm' that must be crossed in order to realize the desired future. Many change efforts fail to achieve expected results because they do not address ways to bridge the 'chasm.' Successfully managing large scale organizational change requires a comprehensive, broad-based approach. To bridge the gap between future and current reality, we need to be explicit about the multiple levels on which we must think and act."[15]

Identifying Barriers and Leverage

One process that can be useful in making the vision real is identifying potential barriers and opportunities in the implementation of the vision. *Force Field Analysis* is a tool that was conceptualized by Kurt Lewin, an American social psychologist and one of the founders of modern psychology. It offers a way to analyze the forces that support change and the forces that undermine change. In his words, "An issue is held in balance by the interaction of two opposing forces – those seeking to promote

---

14 According to the US Labor and Statistics department, every day, more than 12 workers die on the job, over 4,500 a year and every year, more than 4.1 million workers suffer a serious job-related injury or illness. United States Department of Labour. Occupations Safety & Health Administration. Injury Illness Prevention Programs. Washington DC: OSHA: January 2012. https://www.osha.gov/dsg/InjuryIllnessPreventionProgramsWhitePaper.html

15 Kim, Daniel. "The vision deployment matrix."

change (driving forces) and those seeking to maintain the status quo (restraining forces)."[16]

Organizations can be seen as a dynamic balance of forces working in opposite directions. In order for any change to occur, the driving forces must exceed the restraining forces. Work with your team using Force Field Analysis to identify all of the driving and restraining forces that are relevant to the adoption and implementation of the shared vision. This can provide unexpected insight into potential barriers and opportunities as well as levers that you were unaware of before.

After having identified the internal and external forces, teams find it useful to explore how the forces supporting the realization of the shared vision can be strengthened; likewise, thinking creatively about how to reduce the negative effect of those forces which can potentially undermine the realization of the vision. There are a number of websites that describe this tool in detail, including ways to visualize it.

Thinking Creatively About Whose Support/ Acceptance Is Needed

> **In order to gain support and acceptance for the vision, it's critical that you look at it through the eyes of those who will be impacted by it.**

In order to gain support and acceptance for the vision, it's critical that you look at it through the eyes of those who will be impacted by it. But who are all these people? One way to be more certain of this is to invite your team to go through the list of questions in the sidebar, note down their responses, share first with one or two other people, and then the entire group. This increases the likelihood of identifying stakeholders which might not have come to mind initially.

---

16 Kotter, John. *Leading Change.*

Identifying Stakeholders – for Support and Acceptance

- Who, among our stakeholders, customers, distributers, partners, etc., needs to hear and understand our vision?

- Which of these stakeholders need to emotionally and philosophically be aligned with the vision?

- Who are the key players and supporters we believe can motivate others to buy into the vision?

- Who are the people we need to gain acceptance from?

- Who are the persons/groups who will likely support and can assist in making the vision a reality?

- Who are the individuals, groups, departments, etc. that might resist achieving our vision?

The next step is to create a shorter list of key people whose acceptance and support is critical. Invite the team to close their eyes, relax, and imagine that they meet with each of these individuals. Guide them to picture each person in their mind's eye. Where are they? What does each stakeholder look like? How does each one sound? What are you doing and saying as you try to communicate your change vision? How is the stakeholder responding? Guided imagery can be very useful in gaining information about how to facilitate their acceptance of the vision.

In our introductory crisis case study, Marjorie asked the three managers to imagine being the CEO. What kinds of questions might the CEO ask? What would be their concerns? She asked the three managers to imagine being the union leader. What would the union leaders' concerns be? The managers saw themselves meeting with various people and listening to their reactions. This allowed them to address concerns and problems proactively, before they were even raised by their stakeholders.

Taking time to think through and discuss which groups and stakeholders inside and outside the organization need to be informed, which ones you actively need to obtain acceptance from, who might be potential resisters – all of this information is useful. It gives background for being able to tailor approaches to gaining acceptance and support depending on the situation and needs of different types of stakeholders. It will help your team create an informed, proactive and robust plan for reducing the gap between your vision and current reality.

Action Planning

We have reached the action planning point in the process – usually a comfort zone for everyone. We won't belabor this section, but we will offer a couple of builds to the typical action planning process. By combining divergent thinking and guided imagery with action planning, you will find that the outcomes are more specific, detailed, informed and ultimately easier to implement. Select the questions below that are most relevant to your situation and/or write some new ones to cover areas these don't address. Ask participants to jot down their responses, and then invite them to share either in small groups, or in the large group. The ideas that emerge in relation to the questions will naturally funnel into additional action items for the plan.

Questions for Action Planning

- What first steps might we take to initiate action? How? When? Why?

- What next steps might follow? How? When? Where? Why?

- What deadlines or schedules might we follow?

- What resources could be of assistance? How might we best put them to use?

- What follow-up might we need to deal with unexpected repercussions?

- What important obstacles must be considered in implementing the plan?

- What new skills might be critical for achieving our vision?

- In what ways can we ensure that employees can ask questions and offer feedback to our change vision?

- In what ways can we test people's understanding of our vision and its implications in their area of responsibility?

- In what ways can we walk the walk?

- In what ways might we reward behavior?

- In what ways can we ensure that decisions support the achievement of the change vision?

Communicating the Shared Vision

We have included a brief discussion of the importance of communicating the shared vision in this chapter because it is so critically important to the process of making a vision real. It's another step in the process that can benefit tremendously from the use of guided imagery. But before we discuss how to use it in this context, let's first explore some of the best practices for communicating a change vision. Kotter states that, "Clear, simple, memorable, often-repeated, consistent communication from multiple sources, modeled by executive behavior, helps enormously." And, he warns, "Nothing undermines the communication of a change vision more than behavior on the part of key players that seems inconsistent with the vision."[17] He goes on to describe the barriers to adoption of change visions as:

> **Clear, simple, memorable, often-repeated, consistent communication from multiple sources, modeled by executive behavior, helps enormously.**

---

17 Ibid, page 99

- the tendency to under-communicate a change process;

- sending out inconsistent messaging (including not behaving in sync with the vision);

- failing to meaningfully involve stakeholders in digesting and engaging in the change process.

The ability to activate a vision organizationally is not driven by engaging the internal marketing department in sending out emails about the new vision. Instead, it "happens because dozens of managers, supervisors and executives look at all of their daily activities through the lens of the new vision. When people do this, they can easily find many meaningful ways to talk about the direction of change, communications that can always be tailored to the specific person or group with whom they are talking."[18]

There is an often un-discussed but critically important aspect to making the vision real – dealing with the emotional aspects of the changes required by the vision. People immediately want to know, how will this impact me? Who will I report to? What will I have to do differently? Will the change be difficult for me personally? How committed am I to going through difficulties? Helping people work through the emotional aspect of letting go of the status quo, coming to grips with sacrifices, or coming to trust others is hard work that is often not addressed.

Much of the assimilation process happens in one-on-one conversations. Those personal connections create space for a two-way dialogue about the change, allow time to reveal and address personal concerns, and build a sense of connection and trust. Anyone who has been involved in leading or managing change can relate to the idea that people don't hear the change vision clearly, or even at all, the first time. Every communication effort must be treated as though it is your most important attempt at getting

> **Every communication effort must be treated as though it is your most important attempt at getting the message out.**

18 Ibid, page 94

the message out. When your stakeholders finally do hear it, they are likely to consider that it is the first time you have said anything about it. Give people enough time and multiple opportunities to hear and digest the vision.

Many books offer advice on what we would call a more "technical" approach to organizational communication of a change initiative. We think each organization, team or guiding coalition is best served by thinking creatively together about a whole host of possibilities for communicating their vision and deciding which options best serve their purpose.

Key Aspects of an Effective Communication Strategy

- In what ways might we <u>simplify and make the core of our change vision jargon free</u>?

- What are some alternative <u>forms of presenting</u> our vision (e.g., drawings, stories, metaphors, analogies)?

- What are the possible <u>forums for communicating</u> our vision (e.g., social media, off-site retreats, department meetings, one-on-one, podcasts)?

- What are all the possible <u>venues</u> where we can communicate our vision (e.g., office kitchen, cafeteria, meeting rooms, reception area)?

- What <u>channels</u> might we use to communicate our vision (e.g., website, intranet, letterhead, onsite video studio)?

- In which of our <u>existing programs</u> might we communicate our vision (e.g., leadership development programs, introduction to new employees, recruitment interviews, product launch)?

- In what ways can we <u>customize the benefits of the vision</u> to each stakeholder group?

We encourage the team to meet and spend time generating possible solutions related to each aspect. Undoubtedly, you will come up with questions that we haven't included here, so just add them on and apply a similar process.

The Process of Generating Options for Communicating the Vision

- Focus on one aspect of communicating the vision at a time. Defer judgment and aim for quantity. We have provided a few ideas to clarify what is meant, but stretch yourself to come up with as many new and unique possibilities as you can think of. The more options you generate, the greater the likelihood that some of them may be original. Perhaps you will discover connections between ideas and find that together they lead to a new option. In this first phase, avoid all attempts to judge, evaluate or analyze.

- After you feel satisfied that the group has generated a wide variety of ideas, examine each one more carefully. We are quick to focus on what's wrong with an idea or why the idea would never work. Try instead to apply an appreciative approach, focusing on what could work about each one. After identifying the strengths or advantages of an idea, discuss concerns, limitations and weak points. Concerns can be reformulated as a question that opens up opportunities for additional creativity. For example, "How might we . . . ?" The ideas that pop up can strengthen and improve the option.

- Examine all the options for communicating the change vision – selecting, evaluating and refining each so they become workable approaches both short-term and long-term. (We have written in previous chapters about identifying and selecting criteria for evaluating options. You might find that process useful here as well.)

The Importance of Short Term Wins

While effectively communicating the vision is incredibly important, nothing validates it quite as much as short-term wins. When evidence can be given that the vision makes a difference and has positive impacts on work, people, customers or results, even skeptics tend to naturally engage more fully with it.

But why are these short-term wins so important? Change is difficult, no matter how inspired an organization may be. Short-term wins provide reinforcement – they show people that their efforts are making a difference. These kinds of small wins also help to solidify the coalition of support that is needed for success. Leadership buys into the vision more fully and initial skeptics become more open to supporting the vision. The process of producing short-term wins is also valuable in that it begins the process of testing the efficacy of the vision. It opens the door for feedback, reflection and fine tuning or adjusting the vision so that it can be even more motivating.

Kotter[19] describes a good short- term win in the following way:

- It's visible; large numbers of people can see for themselves whether the result is real or just hype.

- It's unambiguous; there can be little argument over the call.

- It's clearly related to the change effort.

Leaders should look for opportunities to communicate and celebrate small successes. New ways of working, interacting with customers, other departments or functions, with the local community, or ideas that have improved processes, products and services should be credited to the employees. Internal publications and news releases should attribute successes to people and teams, not to the "organization" or the "system." Internal publications should make it clear how new projects, programs

19 Ibid, page 121

and progress support visions becoming reality. In crediting people with progress, we reinforce their behaviors and provide them with an opportunity to see how they are responsible for influencing their own future.

> **In crediting people with progress, we reinforce their behaviors and provide them with an opportunity to see how they are responsible for influencing their own future.**

There should be frequent, honest and open discussions about what is or is not working well. Without an ongoing awareness of today's reality, visions lose their power. What forces (behaviors, norms, systems structures, ways of working together, decision-making processes, information flow, and corporate guidelines) are supporting movement in the direction of the vision? Which ones are blocking progress? Which are in conflict? Unless people understand how they are contributing to creating their current reality, they don't see how they can work towards changing that reality. Finally, managers should be evaluated on their commitment to their unit's and organization vision as it is demonstrated through their daily actions and priorities.

There is a lot of work involved in making the shared vision real. But using imagery and creative thinking to implementation and communication planning can provide a more insightful plan, a better approach to communicating with stakeholders and ultimately a more effective roll out. In the conclusion, we'll reflect more deeply on the longer-term impacts and the potential of facilitating change through a whole brain approach to creating shared vision.

Chapter Seven

The Longer-Term Impacts
of Shared Vision

In the Introduction to this book we promised that we would arm you with tools and strategies for facilitating change through the creation of shared visions. We encouraged you to look at visions differently; to think of them as a tool for supporting and enhancing many kinds and levels of change rather than one big end product that describes the whole organization's future. We tried to pique your curiosity about what might be possible in your organization if you were to apply even a small part of the shared visioning process to an opportunity in your company. We hope that we have achieved that.

But, there is a big difference between reading a cookbook and making and eating a new dish! In our quest to motivate you to take a big bite of this content, let's revisit the very compelling "why" around using a shared visioning approach to leading change. There are some fundamental longer-term impacts we have seen over the years. These impacts apply to at the individual, team, function and organizational culture level.

Clarity of Purpose and Creating a Sense of Meaningfulness

> **When leaders and their teams identify critical challenges and thereafter experience their capacity to envision a desired outcome or solution to these challenges, they come in deeper contact with their own, and their organizations', sense of purpose.**

When leaders and their teams identify critical challenges and thereafter experience their capacity to envision a desired outcome or solution to these challenges, they come in deeper contact with their own, and their organizations', sense of purpose. This process helps fulfill the ongoing need for leaders and their teams to derive greater meaning from their work. Their shared visions become the picture of how they see their purpose unfolding as they move into the future. Their actions contribute to the realization of the vision and the fulfillment of purpose. They become more conscious of the choices they need to make in order to serve that purpose.

A recent Fast Company article states that, "Increasing a sense of meaningfulness at work is one of the most potent – and underutilized – ways to increase productivity, engagement, and performance."[20] The article goes on to state that a survey completed by The Energy Project, which reached more than 12,000 employees across a broad range of companies and industries, found that 50% of US employees lack a level of meaning and significance at work. The link between meaningful work and retention is significant; employees who find meaning in their work are three times as likely to stay with their organizations. The survey's findings suggest that meaning trumps items related to learning and growth, connection to a company's mission, and even work-life balance.

---

20 Amortegui, Jessica. "Why finding meaning at work is more important than feeling happy." Fast Company, June 26th 2014. Accessed June 2017. https://www.fastcompany.com/3032126/how-to-find-meaning-during-your-pursuit-ofhappiness-at-work.

Employees who find meaning at work also report 1.7 times higher job satisfaction and are 1.4 times more engaged at work. These are compelling statistics that help to show why employee and stakeholder participation in creating shared visions can have a powerful impact on experiencing a sense of purpose and meaningfulness in today's organizations.

Enhanced Empowerment

Empowerment is a process of enhancing the possibilities for people to gain control over their own lives and to influence the decisions that affect their lives. It involves supporting individuals in developing the competencies, abilities and skills they need to have to perform their work at a high level and have successful interactions with others. It has to do with the capacity to act in accordance with others to fulfill one's potential rather than against others. When we feel empowered, we are willing to take responsibility for our situation, recognizing that we are part of a larger social whole. It means taking responsibility for the success of our work place, unit and company. Participation in creating a shared vision, in developing action plans and taking steps to implement the plan are all powerful steps to enhancing empowerment.

Stronger Alignment and Focus

Creating conditions by which people can feel empowered without creating the focus and alignment provided by a shared vision can lead to an organization without direction. It may produce movement, but without the desired impacts. Creating shared visions around critical organizational challenges helps meet the growing need for alignment and focus. Anyone with a year or two of management or leadership experience can attest to the challenges of getting a team aligned and focused around its most important priorities. A shared vision provides focus. It can be a mechanism for coordinating the efforts of groups with diverging

> A shared vision allows everyone to intuitively grasp the whole — the big picture. It can prevent teams from dissipating their strengths in a variety of unrelated directions.

interests. A shared vision allows everyone to intuitively grasp the whole – the big picture. It can prevent teams from dissipating their strengths in a variety of unrelated directions.

In our experience, people will focus and align around important initiatives when they are given the opportunity to participate in the change in a meaningful way. Creating a shared vision supports the need for stronger alignment and focus.

Increased Commitment

As technology, demographic changes and cost-cutting drive flatter organizational structures, teams must work in more of a collaborative and cross-functional manner. Many of the traditional hierarchal control mechanisms no longer work. And, clearly, they are not the solution for companies striving to develop a more innovative and creative culture. Simultaneously giving greater freedom and expecting greater commitment may seem paradoxical. But a vision, providing it is effectively communicated, easily understood and "alive" in the minds of employees, can replace close supervision. The need for rules is reduced. When it is a vision we believe in, one we ourselves have created or contributed to creating, the potential for real commitment is increased. If our physical, intellectual and emotional energy becomes channeled into something that has greater meaning, we commit to it. The supervision comes from within.

> **If our physical, intellectual and emotional energy becomes channeled into something that has greater meaning, we commit to it. The supervision comes from within.**

Strengthened Climate for Creativity

By helping leaders and teams lean further into their intuitive, creative and imaginative capacities, visionary thinking supports the growth of a much-needed climate for creativity. The ability to be innovative is a primary determinant of business success. Scott Isaksen states that, "There is a general agreement that work environment, and climate for creativity in particular, contributes to organizational performance. Leaders play a crucial role in creating the work environment that either facilitates or inhibits creativity and innovation – critical factors for organizational performance and growth. In fact, some research has indicated that the most important thing leaders can do is create the context for creativity and innovation to flourish."[21]

Participation in creating a powerful mental image of a desired outcome that is different from the reality recognized in the present is not only a meaningful and inspiring creative process, it stimulates a desire to think creatively about how to make the vision today's reality. Since there is no one way of achieving a vision, creativity is constantly spurred on. Teams have to make and communicate meaningful new connections, be able to see new and unusual possibilities, and generate and select from a variety of alternatives. When people experience how they, through their own creativity, can identify new and effective ways to reduce the gap between the vision and current reality, it shifts their own mindsets and strengthens their belief in their ability to find creative solutions.

As the powerful mental images of a desired future state becomes closer to reality, there is a need to create another desired future state. The vision and the present reality are always in tension, but in a healthy way. This means we are always creating the future with the intention of developing further, of serving a higher purpose. This promotes ongoing creative thinking; it becomes a habit. Learning and experience continually reinforce the ability to resolve organizational and leadership challenges, allowing organizations to perpetually reinvent their futures. It's a virtuous cycle that continually drives growth in the capacity for creative thinking and innovation.

Visions are not somewhere out in space. They do not reside in the air, or as a statement or drawing in a brochure. Visions are alive and real in the minds of those visioning. Our experience with facilitating change through

21 Isaksen, S.G. "Leadership's role in creative climate creation." In Handbook of research on leadership and creativity, M.D. Mumford & S. Hemlin (eds.), 131-158. Northampton, MA: Edward Elgar, 2017.

shared vision has convinced us that individual and organizational spirit is nurtured and strengthened by being in touch with values, having a clear sense of purpose and a compelling vision towards which actions are directed. Leaders who engage their teams in identifying critical challenges and involving them in envisioning solutions to these challenges don't need to be told to be more change oriented. They are taking responsibility for change. Their attention is focused on what they want to create and not on becoming change oriented.

> **Leaders who engage their teams in identifying critical challenges and involving them in envisioning solutions to these challenges don't need to be told to be more change oriented. They are taking responsibility for change.**

All of these longer-term impacts of facilitating change through shared visioning are powerful leadership and culture builders. They impact organizations positively on multiple levels and layers. They equip organizations with leaders and employees who can more effectively lead for an innovative future. We hope that now, having read this book, you are inspired to discover for yourself how creating shared visions can positively impact your organization's ability to address the critical challenges it faces.

About the Authors

Marjorie Parker is an organizational consultant who has been recognized for over 30 years as a thought leader in the field of creativity. A native of Rochester, Minnesota, Marjorie resides in Oslo, Norway. She has consulted with senior management in Norway's leading corporations, healthcare institutions and government agencies. She has developed and led training programs for internal and external consultants in applying creative approaches to strategy development and organizational change. She was founding partner in the consulting company, the Norwegian Center for Leadership Development.

Marjorie was awarded a national scholarship from the Norwegian Council for Leadership Development and was a recipient of a stipend from the Norwegian Council for Scientific and Industrial Research to document work using innovative approaches to leadership development and organizational change. She holds an M.Sc. from the International Center for Studies in Creativity, Buffalo, NY.

Marjorie is the author of the book *Creating Shared Vision – The Story of a Pioneering Approach to Organizational Revitalization*, published in the US, Poland, Norway and Saudi Arabia. Peter Senge, author of the wildly acclaimed book *The Fifth Discipline*, wrote the following in the foreword: "The story told in *Creating Shared Vision* is fascinating. It should be mandatory reading for those interested in revitalizing their organizations and in moving toward becoming learning organizations." Marjorie is also the co-author of the book *Dialogue – A Practical Guide* published in 2012 in Norwegian, in Oslo, Norway.

Today, Marjorie focuses on mentoring organizational consultants who are searching for new ways to develop a more creative mindset within their own client organizations.

Anna Pool is a business consultant and strategic thinker who has facilitated leadership and organizational development across a broad range of industries and clients, including Michelin, Shell, Verizon, Citi, Bayer, Nike, Raytheon and the Ford Motor Company, as well as numerous government agencies. A master-level certified executive coach with the Association of Corporate Executive Coaches, she is a trusted advisor to top leadership, providing insight, tough feedback and helping leaders build innovative and collaborative environments where the desired future state can be envisioned and systematically enabled.

She is president of Executive Savvy, [executivesavvyinc.com], a boutique consulting firm headquartered in Durango, Colorado. Her business background includes experience at the Director and Board level of an alternative health care facility, benchmarked by the Harvard Medical School as one of the most innovative and effective of its kind. She is the former Director of Organizational Consulting for Lore International Institute (now a Korn Ferry company). She also served as the organizational learning consultant for Ford's New Business Leader program, an innovative action-learning program that was benchmarked by the International Consortium on Executive Development as among the best in the world.

Anna is the author of the Bronze Telly Award-winning video series, *Effective People Skills*, and is the co-author of Lore's 360 *Assessment of Collaborative Tendencies*. She holds a Master's degree in Organizational Development from the Fielding Institute in Santa Barbara, CA. and has completed a two-year certification with The Gestalt Institute of the Berkshires.

Acknowledgements

The authors are grateful to so many people who provided both practical and personal support in the creation of this book.

Zoë Harris, our fearless editor, whose support has been invaluable in our ability to share this work with the world. Kate Coe of Scritto Editing provided additional editing and proofreading, ensuring our work was articulate and cohesive.

"Tusen takk" (Norwegian for a thousand thanks) to Tresa Gowland who graciously coached us through the process of making the presentation of the book more professional and elevated the look and feel of the book along with Andrew Kim, our cover illustrator and graphic designer. Home run, Andrew! Let's just leave it as "we were clueless". Julie Gordon, Graphic Designer, provided us with early graphic templates helping us to think visually.

A very special thank you to Gerd Stykket, Juanita Brown and Brit Opjordsmoen, who read our entire manuscript and provided insightful feedback, asked important questions and encouraged us. Your guidance was fundamental in keeping us on track.

Our spirits were lifted and our resolve strengthened by the generosity of our early readers who read portions of the draft manuscript, shared their insights and unequivocally told us to keep going. A huge thank-you to Deirdre Fay, Dr. Don Stapleton, Jack Rotundi, Joy Lubeck, Barbara Spencer Singer, Suzanne-Ann Stämpfli, Geir Lieblein, Gidske Holck, Christina Tønnesen and Dag Olav Norem.

Finally, friends and family, thank you for believing in the importance of this work. You were there in those not-so-inspired moments to provide the encouragement to keep believing and keep writing.

Bibliography

Amortegui, Jessica. "Why finding meaning at work is more important than feeling happy." *Fast Company*, June 26th 2014. Accessed June 2017.
https://www.fastcompany.com/3032126/
how-to-find-meaning-during-your-pursuit-ofhappiness-at-work

Axner, Marya. *Leadership and Management*. Kansas: University of Kansas. Accessed June 2017.
http://ctb.ku.edu/en/table-of-contents/leadership/
leadership-functions/develop-and-communicate-vision/main

Bolte Taylor, Jill. "My Stroke of Insight". TED Talk, TED 2008. Accessed June 2017.
https://www.ted.com/talks/
jill_bolte_taylor_s_powerful_stroke_of_insight

Dweek, Carol: *Mindset: The New Psychology of Success*. New York: Ballentine Books, 2006.

"Force Field Analysis: Analysing the pressures for and against change." *MindTools*, no date. Accessed June 2017.
https://www.mindtools.com/pages/article/newTED_06.htm

Isaksen, S.G. "Leadership's role in creative climate creation." In *Handbook of research on leadership and creativity*, M.D. Mumford & S. Hemlin (eds.), 131-158. Northampton, MA: Edward Elgar, 2017.

Kim, Daniel. "The vision deployment matrix – a framework for large scale change". *The Systems Thinker*, accessed June 2017. https://thesystemsthinker.com/ vision-deployment-matrix-aframework-for-large-scale-change/

Kotter, John P. "How to create a powerful vision for change". *Forbes*, June 7th 2011. Accessed June 2017. http://www.forbes.com/sites/johnkotter/2011/06/07/ how-to-create-a-powerfulvision-for-change/#4cfc40fd2a3c

Kotter, John P. *Leading Change.* Boston, MA: Harvard Business School Press, 1996.

Moss Kanter, Rosabeth. *Change Masters.* New York: Free Press, 1985.

Parker, Marjorie. *Creating Shared Vision – the story of a pioneering approach to organizational revitalization.* Clarendon Hills, Ill: Dialog International Ltd, 1990.

Parker, Marjorie. *Sammen om visjoner-Et pionerarbeid om nytenkning i praksis.* Oslo: Hjemmets bokforlag AS, 1992.

Pehrson, John B. and Mehrtens, Susan E. *Intuitive Imagery – a Resource at Work.* Newton, MA: Butterworth-Heinemann, 1997.

Schwartz, Andrew E. *Guided Imagery for Groups.* Duluth, MN: Whole Person Associates, Inc., 1995.

United States Department of Labour. Occupations Safety & Health Administration. *Injury Illness Prevention Programs.* Washington DC: OSHA: January 2012. https://www.osha.gov/dsg/ InjuryIllnessPreventionProgramsWhitePaper.html

Appendix

Appendix 1: Relaxation exercises

Before you move into your actual script for the visioning process, be sure to lead one of the relaxation exercises we have included below. You'll find they are great exercises any time you want to increase your level of focus, calm your nervous system or connect with a quieter place inside.

Note that you will move directly from the relaxation exercise into the visioning script without debriefing or asking people to open their eyes. This ensures that the team can stay in a quiet and creative mindset for the visioning.

There are a variety of ways to relax and different people have different preferences.

Relaxation #1: Counting Breaths

Instructions: To become relaxed we are going to spend a few minutes counting breaths. Try to follow my counting instructions, but you should never strain or struggle to hold your breath. If it feels difficult at any point or if you feel dizzy, simply lessen the amount of time you inhale, hold and exhale.

Close your eyes, and on take a slow, deep breath to the count of one . . . two . . . three . . . four, and then hold it to the count of one . . . two . . . three . . . four, and then exhale to the count of one . . . two . . . three . . . four. Inhale again to the count of one . . . two . . . three . . . four, and then hold it to the count of one . . . two . . . three . . . four, and then exhale to the count of one . . . two . . . three . . . four.

Continue now to count to yourself and as you inhale, imagine you are inhaling fresh air from a natural setting that you love. It might in the mountains [pause] it could be by the ocean [pause] or even your own back yard. Just imagine someplace you feel relaxed. And each time you exhale, you are letting go of any tension, any tiredness, anything that might be distracting you from enjoying this moment. [Continue with this breathing for about 5 minutes.]

Now I am going to guide you into the vision for your desired future state. Please keep your eyes closed as we transition together.

Relaxation # 2: Body-Centered Relaxation

Instructions: Let's start by getting comfortable. Rub your hands together to create some heat and then press your hands to your face and give yourself a little face rub.

[Pause.]

Then, gently close your eyes or fix your gaze on something directly in front of you. Become aware of your breathing. I'm going to slowly guide you on a journey where you can gradually relax all the parts of your body. Let's begin with your feet. Squeeze your toes a few times and become aware of the energy that flows into them as you do that simple movement. Take a deep breath and sigh out any tension in your feet. Then become aware of your calves. Tighten your calf muscles and release them several times, feeling the flow of energy increase to your lower legs. Then become aware of your thighs, those large muscles that allow you to move powerfully through the world. Tighten and then release those muscles, feeling the increase of energy flowing through them.

Now notice your buttock muscles, feel your sitz bones pressing into the chair. Become aware of your pelvis and groin, and take some deep breaths into this area of the body, just noticing the flow of energy that is created by your breath, your awareness. Move your awareness up to your belly, take some deep breaths way down into the belly area. Sigh out any tension you may be holding there and bring awareness to the warmth that is created as you focus there.

Now bring your awareness up to your chest, your heart, your lungs, allowing your breath to deepen even further. Try to really empty your lungs with each exhalation. If you feel dizzy just return to normal breathing, but try to really focus here, feeling the energy relax, energize and heal your entire torso. Now bring your awareness to your shoulders and arms, sending the breath all the way down your arms to your fingertips. Stay there and breathe, allow the breath to bring you back to the sensations in your body, leaving the mental chatter behind, over and over again.

Finally, bring your attention up through your neck through the back of your head, across the crown of the head and then down into the forehead, eyes, ears, nose, cheeks and mouth. Keep breathing there until you can feel a gentle flow of energy relaxing your brain, your face, your neck and your throat.

Appendix 2: Exercises for practicing imagery

As we pointed out in Chapter One, visionary thinking is about imaging the future. It's about bringing new possibilities into being. There may be people in your team who easily admit that they regularly day dream while sitting at their office desk or have no problem fantasizing about feeling the warm sun on a sandy beach, but who do not believe that they are able to image being in a desired future state. We have found that introducing some simple and fun imagery exercises before getting started with visionary thinking around an important organizational challenge helps people who are in doubt about their own ability to image to feel more comfortable with the process. Choose one of these exercises as an introductory exercise. If you don't think they are the right fit for your group, we suggest you do an Internet search for "guided imagery," where you will find numerous websites that offer suggestions for simple start-up exercises.

Let's review a few facts about imagery: Imagery is the mental processes of creating sights, sounds, smells, tastes and sensations in the absence of any actual external stimuli. Imagery is a means of improving communication between the conscious and unconscious levels of the mind as it provides simultaneous access to both levels. Our images give us the power to span time. An image held in the mind can affect every cell in the body. Images are a vehicle for profound intuitive insights. Imagery allows us to express ideas and feelings which are not usually easily accessible. It is an especially useful tool when dealing with tasks that are complex, uncertain and novel, such as envisioning a desired future state. Guided imagery is the process of leading someone on an imagery journey. A facilitator suggests a theme and the imager creates a corresponding image.

Imaging Practice #1: Imagine an Extraordinary Chair

Start by imagining that you are standing in front of a door. [pause] Then imagine yourself slowly opening the door, and what you see, standing alone in the middle of the room is an extraordinary chair! [pause]

See yourself walk towards this chair, stand and look at it, [pause]. Maybe it has features you have never seen before. [pause] Now, walk in a circle around it and notice how it looks from different angles. [pause] With one hand reach out and touch it. What material is it made from?

[pause] What color is it? [pause]

Now, gently sit down in the chair and notice how your back, your arms and your legs feel as you relax into it. [pause] And now imagine one of your favorite pieces of music, any kind of music is fine, begins to waft slowly into the room. Let the music fill the room allow yourself to just enjoy it. [pause] Take a brief rest here, listening to your music. [pause]

Now it's time to get out of your chair and slowly walk back to the door, leaving the chair for now.

Gently open your eyes and turn to one other person on the team take turns describing your chair to each other.

Imaging Practice #2: Design a Glass[22]

This is a fun exercise that gives people an opportunity to experience their own creative imagination through sensory images. It takes 6-8 minutes. Every participant should have an ordinary drinking glass on the table in front of them.

Inhale and exhale slowly and completely three times. One . . . [pause for five seconds], two . . . [pause for five seconds] Three . . . [pause for five seconds]. Continue this easy, relaxed breathing.

Pick up your drinking glass and examine it closely. Notice how solid and clear it is. Study the glass until you have its shape and mass clearly in your mind. Notice how it catches the light, especially inside the gently curved bottom.

---

22 Schwartz, A. *Guided Imagery for Groups.*

Concentrate on the glass, and now put it down on the table in front of you [pause for five seconds]. Now close your eyes and recall the image of the glass [pause for five seconds].

Now that the glass is in your mind, you are going to mold it as if it were soft, clear clay.

You can stretch it vertically . . . or horizontally . . .

Add decorations . . . or a wider base . . . or squeezed middle . . . or a fancy handle . . . whatever you wish.

Move deliberately and carefully . . . impose each adjustment slowly . . .

And after each change, re-examine the glass. If you don't like the result, try something else.

Once you have designed the shape of your glass. You are ready to engrave something on its inner surface.

The message should appear rough and cloudy. Whiter than the rest of the glass.

You could etch your name, or someone else's. Or a short message such as coffee . . . or tea . . . or any message or design you choose.

After the glass has been engraved, study it until you feel that it is permanent.

[Pause for 20 seconds.]

Now fill your glass with a liquid. And notice how that liquid colors the glass. If your glass is thicker in certain places than in others, notice how that affects the apparent color of the liquid. [Pause for 20 seconds.]

Now, put a clear straw into the glass of liquid. Once the straw has settled, change its appearance. Give it a solid color or two. Make it candy-striped or polka-dotted. You might change its length and shape.

[Pause for 15 seconds.]

Again, make sure that once you have chosen a design for your straw. Study it long enough to give it permanence.

[Pause for 10 seconds.]

Finally, if you choose, you may drink the liquid. Remember that you can adjust its taste and temperature. You may decide to have it hot or cold, sweet or bitter, tangy, carbonated or anything else.

[Pause for 10 seconds.]

Think now about how satisfying and thirst-quenching the liquid is.

And as you think about the liquid, you have completed the last step. It is now time for you to awaken and open your eyes.

Feel how refreshed your body is now [pause] how relaxed [pause] how peaceful you feel.

Prepare yourself to return to the room on the count of three. One . . . two . . . three . . .

Afterwards: Share your glass design visualization experience with a partner and reflect how it felt to be creative!

Imagery Practice #3: Reconstruction of a House

Imagine that you are walking down a small road just outside of town when suddenly you come across an old abandoned house.

[Pause]

Stop in front of this house and notice that the garden is overgrown and full of weeds. Some windows are broken and even a wall looks like it might soon collapse.

[Pause]

Open the creaking, wooden front door, go in, and look at the empty, dusty rooms.

[Pause]

The sight of this abandoned house and its uncultivated garden may give you a sense of sadness. But, think of what this house could become if you decided to fix it up!

Now tell yourself, "I'm going to fix it up!"

[Pause]

Decide to start inside the house. Imagine that all the tools you need are available to you and that you have all the skills that are necessary.

[Pause]

So, begin with the walls. Wherever you see a wall that needs repair, start to repair it.

[Pause]

And now repair the roof where needed.

[Pause]

Replace the rusty hinges of the doors with new ones.

[Pause]

Where the floorboards are rotten, replace them, too.

[Pause]

Put new glass in the broken windows.

[Pause]

Begin to paint the living room area and the dining area.

[Pause]

And now paint the kitchen in exactly the color that you think is best.

[Pause]

The living room, dining area and kitchen are ready to be furnished. Imagine tables and chairs, bookcases and paintings and others things you would like to have in these rooms. It is your house and you can furnish it just as you like. Take your time and furnish each of these rooms.

[Pause]

Go outside now and begin to weed the garden and turn over the earth in preparation for planting. When the soil is ready, sow seeds of various flowers in different parts of the garden according to the picture you have in mind of how the garden will look in full bloom. Clean the house. Paint the inside walls and outside walls. What colors are you choosing?

The time has come to put life and energy in the house. Check the water supply and see that it flows properly. Put some food in the refrigerator in the kitchen. Walk in the garden and notice that the plants are already beginning to blossom. They are of many colors and many shapes.

Look at them all and smell them.

Pick some flowers and put them in vases.

[Pause]

Now, go stand outside on the lawn several meters away from the house and admire the work you have done. Notice that the garden is in full bloom.

[Pause]

At your own tempo, gradually open your eyes.

Appendix 3: Scripts for fast forwarding to the future

The Electronic Calendar on Your Computer

Instructions: "Imagine yourself sitting at your desk back at your office. You are looking at the electronic calendar on your monitor, which is showing this month, including today's date of [for example June 1st, 2018]. As you are looking at it, all by itself, the month at the top of the calendar begins to advance, one month at a time. Soon, you see that it is December 1st , 2018, and then suddenly June 1st, 2019. Then it advances again and it is December 1, 2019. And now it begins advancing even more quickly. You see now it's already June of 2020. Suddenly it begins turning very fast as it advances to June of 2021, and then to June of 2022, and then . . . it suddenly stops. As you look down, you see that calendar shows June 1st, 2023, five years from today [or the dates according to your time frame]."

The Changing Seasons

"Picture yourself sitting quietly somewhere in your company's building where there is a window to the outside world. It might be a window in your personal office, it might be the window in the lunch room or an empty conference room. [If this is not realistic, invite the participants to sit by a window in their home or favorite vacation place.] Find a place by a window and make yourself comfortable just looking out of it."

Next, begin to describe the season that is currently underway. We'll use winter as a starting point in this example. Obviously, you will want to make your season geographically appropriate for the location of the team.

"As you gaze out of the window, begin to notice details of the current season. Today is a cold, snowy day. You're glad you dressed warmly as the temperature is supposed to drop later in the day. You look at your watch and notice today's date is February 1, 2018. Then, as you look back out the window, allow the scene in front of you to blur just a bit and suddenly you notice that the view has shifted to spring. The sun is coming out, flowers and trees outside the window are starting to bloom. Take a deep breath and enjoy that spring weather, then let the scene blur again. Now it's summer. You can see people outside wearing summer clothes, eating ice cream, enjoying the hot weather. Now let the picture blur once more. You see that the leaves are turning, people are wearing warmer clothing, there is a nip of frost in the air. You let the scene blur once more and you realize you are back to the winter weather again, but this time, as you look down at your watch, you realize it is February 1, 2019."

CPSIA information can be obtained
at www.ICGtesting.com
Printed in the USA
BVOW11s1004061117

499662BV00024B/1209/P